Chronicle of the Seventh Son
Black Panther Mark Clark

By

Rose (Clark) Morris

Copyright, 2019, by
Rose (Clark) Morris

All rights reserved. Published in the United States of America. No part of this book may be saved or reproduced in any form, or by any means, except for the inclusion of brief quotations in a review, without permission in writing from the author and publisher. Rose (Clark) Morris is the author of this work and all rights are asserted by her in coordination with The Copyright Act of 1976 and subsequent amendments. This book is a nonfiction memoir. It reflects the author's recollections of experiences and stories told to her over time. While all of the events and characters described herein are true, some events have been compressed, and some dialogue has been recreated. This work is sold with the understanding that neither the author nor the publishers are held responsible for any adverse interpretations of the situations described and language used herein. The subject matter found within may not be suitable for every situation. Address inquiries to the author's email, Chronicleseventhson2019@yahoo.com.

ISBN 978 1-7335817-14
Manufactured in the United States of America

TABLE OF CONTENTS

Acknowledgements	7
Forward	11
Introduction	15
Chapter 1. Great Migration from the South	20
Chapter 2. Family Life, Work and Religion	40
Chapter 3. Servant Leadership and Elementary Education	60
Chapter 4. Mark's Early Teens - An Introduction to Activism	88
Chapter 5. Movements, Empowerment and Police	118
Chapter 6. The Year That Was 1968	140
Chapter 7. Mark Clark Joins The Black Panther Party	158
Chapter 8. The December 4th Raid and Assassinations	182

Chapter 9. Media, Misinformation and Investigations	194
Chapter 10. Thirteen Years of Trials and Appeals	204
Chapter 11. Clark Family Values and Moving Forward	215
Chapter 12. Memorials, Tributes and Love Letters	233
About The Author	256
References	262

Acknowledgements

Chronicle of the Seventh Son, Black Panther Mark Clark is a Special Memorial Tribute Book to my strong family unit. Elder William and Mother Fannie Mae Clark were excellent parents. Without them, there would not be a story to tell. They shared many of their experiences of earlier times in Mississippi, Alabama, Tennessee, and Illinois. The stories they shared motivated me to document their information. As a 50th Year Memorial Tribute, this book tells the story of the Clark's and their seventh son, Mark Clark. My beloved brother Mark transitioned from this life as a martyr at twenty-two years old. His dedication to activism, his revolutionary ideals, leadership in the Black Panther Party, and his assassination by government conspiracy were historic events. His willingness to live, struggle, and die for the people is what inspired me to write this book. Thank you, Momma, Daddy, and Mark.

Special acknowledgments go to my husband, Brian E. Morris; daughter, Jaclyn (Clark) Hodge and my niece Melissa Clark.

They provided enthusiasm and sustained assistance. During our many days together their listening ears, book content suggestions, and our numerous cups of coffee motivated me to continue the work. The book would not have been completed if it was not for them. Thank you, Brian, Jaclyn, and Melissa.

My brother, Matthew Clark shared with me his personal recollections and letter of poetry. Matt provided valuable insight and useful information. Thank you, Matt.

My sister, Dr. Patricia (Clark) Lewis contributed her personal recollections and family photographs. Pat inspired me throughout my entire life and motivated me to turn my vision for the book into a reality. Even when obstacles to publication seemed formidable, Patricia's numerous monetary gifts allowed me to continue to pursue the dream of telling the family story. I am extremely thankful to you, Pat.

My sisters, Elner Clark and Gloria (Clark) Jackson, and brothers, Luke Clark, John Clark, and Robert Clark allowed me to glean the benefits of their knowledge over the years. They were valuable resources for the book.

Thank you, Elner, Glo, Luke, Johnny and Robert.

My children, Jaclyn (Clark) Hodge, Phil Hodge, Marcus Hodge, and Aaron Hodge, and my grandchildren, Perry, Paris, Peru, Porsche, Isaiah, and Remi. Thank you all for your support and inspiration.

My niece Dionne Thomas and nephew Calvin Lewis, Jr. provided me with access to old family photographs, and important historical documents that were valuable resources. They showed me hospitality and gave much encouragement and useful advice. Thank you, Dionne and Cal.

To my extended Clark family members that gave their listening ears and support for the project. Thank you, Clark family.

To all the persons named here, I am sincerely grateful.

Forward

Mark Clark had the tenacity to engage in a revolutionary struggle for justice and human rights. He joined the Black Panther Party at a time when they were deemed by FBI officials to be the number one threat to the security of the nation. Mark organized the Peoria, Illinois Chapter of the Black Panther Party and implemented community-based programs in the inner-city. Among the most prominent programs established by his Peoria, Illinois Chapter was the Black Panther Party Free Breakfast Program. When other so-called revolutionaries were dropping out of the struggle, he remained resolute. Mark exhibited tremendous loyalty and courage, even in his final hours. Mark Clark's assassination, along with Chairman Fred Hampton Sr. Leader of the Chicago Chapter of the Black Panther Party cemented his legacy among the Vanguard of the Revolution.

Black Panther Party Leaders, Mark Clark and Chairman Fred Hampton Sr. were assassinated in Chicago, Illinois on December 4th, 1969. The Panther Leaders were murdered in a pre-dawn raid perpetrated by Chicago Police, Cook County States Attorney's Office, and other government conspirators. Over the years, numerous articles and books were written about the Black Panther Party and the infamous December 4th, 1969 raid. Few of these stories focused on Mark Clark's life and his contributions to the Black Power Liberation Struggle. This book entitled *Chronicle of the Seventh Son, Black Panther Mark Clark* is the true story of the activist and revolutionary.

The author, Rose (Clark) Morris is the sister of the slain Black Panther Party Leader. In 1969, Rose was a young girl with a front row seat to history. From her unique vantage point, she watched as her brother and other family members participated in the Civil Rights Movement and the Black Power Liberation Struggle. As a child, she experienced the trauma of her brother's assassination and the deaths of their father, sister, and grandmother. Each death occurred during the turbulent period between 1968 and 1970. Rose never forgot the experiences of her childhood. Eventually, she became determined to tell the family story. She documented her own recollection of events and accounts told to her by their parents and siblings years ago. She interviewed family members for their stories, compiling family photos and historical information. She spent years researching books, articles, and records pertaining to The Black Panther Party, the December 4th raid, and the various court proceedings. *Chronicle of the Seventh Son, Black Panther Mark Clark* brings together the author's research and summarizes it plainly.

Rose (Clark) Morris tells the story of her brother's life growing up in Peoria, Illinois. She describes specific events and interactions with the most influential people in his life. The author provides readers with an insightful look into the characteristics and values of Mark Clark's strong family unit. She shares the story of their father who was an Elder Pastor in the Church of God in Christ and their mother, a Missionary and Poet.

Mark's sister shares the story of her brother's recruitment into The Black Panther Party and his organization of the Peoria, Illinois Chapter. The author exposes the infiltration of the Chicago Chapter of The Black Panther Party, the planning of the December 4th, 1969 raid, and the FBI COINTELPRO conspiracy. She examines the orchestrated media misinformation campaign designed to discredit the Panthers. The book provides readers with a summary review of the Blue Ribbon Coroner's Inquest and the Grand Juries convened. Details of the civil rights lawsuit filed and the thirteen year battle in the courts are included.

Chronicle of the Seventh Son, Black Panther Mark Clark is a gripping account of how a strong African American family dealt with injustice and adversity during some of the most turbulent times of the twentieth century. It is a story that is part of the African American experience. It is a must read story whose time has finally come!

Introduction

Mark Clark was William and Fannie Mae Clark's seventh son. He was born June 28, 1947 the ninth child out of their seventeen children. Mark's parents and siblings would be very influential in his life. They would provide him with a thorough education of religious principles and practices; and knowledge of what was happening in the world.

During Mark's early years, his father was among the most influential figures in his life. Elder William Clark Sr. was a well-known religious leader and highly regarded in the local community. He was Elder Pastor at Lincoln Avenue Church of God in Christ and he served as Superintendent of the Greater Central Illinois District of the COGIC. Elder Clark also served as President of the Interdenominational Ministers Alliance. In 1966, Elder William Clark Sr. founded Holy Temple Church of God in Christ in Peoria, Illinois. He was an exceptionally hard-working man and he labored more than twenty-eight years in the Foundry of Caterpillar Tractor Company in East Peoria, Illinois.

As a child, Mark would sit in the church pews among his other siblings and watch as Elder Clark preached and carry out church ministry. Mark observed his father exhibiting leadership in the church and showing genuine concern for the people.

Mark's mother was a woman of great faith. Fannie Mae Clark was a Missionary and Evangelist in the Church of God in Christ. Mother Clark was a loving wife and mother and she was always showing concern for the well-being of her family and community. She was a woman full of wisdom and knowledge. She loved reading, writing, reciting poetry, and telling bible stories. During Mark's childhood, his mother would tell him stories of defeating enemies, establishing kingdoms, and trampling down evil with determination, courage, and by the power of God.

Mother Fannie Mae Clark played a huge role in inspiring her children to continuously educate themselves. She purchased numerous volumes of the latest encyclopedias which she read from cover to cover. Mother Clark's collection of encyclopedias and reference books were accessed frequently by the entire Clark family. Mark utilized them to educate himself about many of his favorite subjects.

As Mark Clark grew older and began to question the status quo, his siblings became very influential. Mark's older brothers educated him about what was happening in the world and the atmosphere of conflict that existed. His older siblings would engage in debates about such topics as religion, politics, war, colonialism, and racism. They would discuss the plight of black people all over the world. The frequent incidents of racial injustice occurring all across the nation were deeply concerning topics of discussion.

Mark observed how his older siblings began responding to injustice. During the early 1960's, he watched his older brothers protesting with the NAACP. He would listen to his older brothers and other grassroots activists talking about Black Power. They began demanding equal rights, better housing, jobs, and freedom. It was a platform that resonated in Mark's ears. He became inspired to join the NAACP while in his early teens. Several years later, he would make a commitment to engage in a revolutionary struggle for justice and liberation in the Black Panther Party.

Chronicle of the Seventh Son, Black Panther Mark Clark is the story of Mark Clark's life, death, and contributions to the Black Power Liberation Struggle. It is the story of a quintessential revolutionary and his strong family unit. It begins during the early 1900's when Mark Clark's parents and their relatives experienced atrocities of lynching and other despicable acts perpetrated on black people.

Chapter 1

Great Migration from the South

Great Migration from the South

It was on Christmas Day 1929, when William Clark and Fannie Mae Bardley united in holy matrimony. William, then 21 years old; was a tall handsome man with a charismatic personality. He was from the Dancy area in Cochran, Alabama and was born January 16, 1908. Fannie Mae was 14 years old when she married William. She was tall, beautiful, and wise beyond her years. She was born on January 6, 1914 in Robinsonville, Mississippi.

Both William and Fannie Mae Clark were descendants of enslaved African Americans. Their ancestors were forced to work in the cotton fields and tobacco plantations along the black prairie land of Eastern Mississippi and Western Alabama. Fannie Mae's great grandparents, Dallas and Melinda Brewer had ties to the area since the 1840's and died there years back. After emancipation, the Brewer's children and relatives continued to farm the land spanning from the Tombigbee River to its primary tributary, Black Warrior River; named for the Mississippian Paramount Chief Tuscaloosa.

Dallas and Melinda Brewer's children were Fannie Brewer, Ella Davis, Belle Brewer, Willis Brewer, Travis Brewer, Melinda Jane Brewer, and Alex Henry Brewer. Their families were mostly sharecroppers but eventually some were fortunate enough to own land and businesses.

William and Fannie Mae's families understood the importance of the family remaining together despite the negative forces that threatened them. After the Civil War, the government's failure to reconstruct the nation and protect the rights of black people, led to the rise of the klu klux klan. The klan began terrorizing the black masses throughout the south. Some African Americans that owned property had it taken or were harassed and ran off. Many African Americans were jailed on unfair charges and some forced to work on chain gangs. Thousands of black men, women, and children were lynched by angry white mobs. By the early 1900's, William and Fannie Mae's families uprooted themselves from the prairie lands that they long called home.

Fannie Mae's grandmother, Fannie Brewer was matriarch of her branch of the

Brewer family. Fannie Brewer was affectionately known as Maw Fannie. She and her nine children; Ella Terrell, Lottie Brewer, Lela, Lillie Mae, Elner, George, Willie, Travis, and Lucious McNeese all left the Eastern Mississippi towns of Prairie Point and Macon in 1913. It was the year before the First World War began. The family moved to the northern part of Mississippi, settling in the small town of Robinsonville.

In 1916, Fannie Mae's father, Samuel Bardley died unexpectedly. The reason for his death has remained a mystery but the experience left her mother, Ella (Terrell) Bardley a grieving widow. Maw Fannie Brewer stepped in to help raise Fannie Mae. She became her primary caregiver during her childhood years.

Meanwhile, William Clark's father, Alex Clark Sr. settled his family in Tunica, Mississippi, not too far from Robinsonville. Alex and Rena (Hullum) Clark moved their family right next door to his mother, Caroline Conner and his sister Mattie Cochran. Alex Clark Sr. went to the Military Registration Office in Tunica and signed a World War I Draft Registration card in 1917.

During the 1920's, William Clark worked on a levee at the Mississippi River near Robinsonville. His co-worker Robert Williams was also from Alabama and they became friends. At the time, Robert was engaged to Lillie Mae McNeese, who was Fannie Mae's aunt. Lillie Mae and Fannie Mae were more like sisters than aunt and niece. They were only three years apart in age and grew up in the same household headed by Maw Fannie Brewer. William accompanied Robert on his visits to see his fiancée and that's when William met Fannie Mae.

William Clark's light skin caused some people to question whether he was black or not. Census records seemed to go back and forth as to whether his family was black or mulatto. The truth of the matter is both William's grandmothers were African, born enslaved. They were victimized by white men resulting in their conceiving so-called mulatto children. William's father, Alex Clark Sr. was considered a mulatto and so was his mother, Rena (Hullum) Clark. It meant no difference to Fannie Mae whether William's complexion was light-skin or not; as long as his attitude was consistent with the values she held. He identified himself as a black man and took pride in his African ancestral roots. The Clark's understood that the various shades of black people came about as a result of heredity and oppression.

William Clark

Fannie Mae and William Clark

Fannie Mae and William Clark were married on Christmas day. Two years earlier, on Christmas day Lillie Mae McNeese and Robert Williams married. With Fannie Mae and Lillie Mae's sisterly bond, and with William and Robert's shared love of hunting; they would maintain close friendships throughout their lives. As a young couple starting out during the depression era, William and Fannie Mae Clark relied on their relatives and close neighbors.

Times were hard back then but most black people, especially in the south; were familiar with hard times. The Clark's and their relatives survived by farming the land and reaping what it yielded. They grew vegetables like greens, beans, okra, cucumbers, beats, and squash. They raised farm animals mostly chickens. When Fannie Mae recalled of those times she would say "If you needed a cup of sugar, you could go next door and get it from your neighbor; and if you had eggs or milk, you gave it to your neighbor". The Clark's, their relatives, and neighbors shared what they had and helped each other make ends meet.

William and Fannie Mae had a large circle of extended family and friends. The Clark's were close to William's younger siblings, Tommie, Jimmy, Joseph, Johnny, Annie, Mary, Mattie, Alex Clark Jr., Anna Lee (Clark) Mabry, and Irene (Clark) Howard. They also had close-knit relationships with Fannie Mae's extended family members and her mother's numerous siblings. Among them were Lillie Mae and her husband, Robert Williams, Travis McNeese (known as Uncle Bae Bae), and Elner (McNeese) Partlow Blackburn who was called by the nickname, Aintee.

Elner Partlow Blackburn was tall, outspoken, and rambunctious. In her youth, she was considered to be one of the most beautiful girls in Tunica County, Mississippi. She married in her teenage years but her young husband was among the hundreds of black men lynched by white mobs in Tunica. His lynching traumatized her and affected the entire family adding to their mistrust of many white people.

Travis McNeese was a sensitive man who was the youngest of Fannie Mae's mother's siblings. He worked as a Porter on the railroad trains. The job was considered prestigious for a black man. The Pullman Porters were at the forefront fighting for better pay and working conditions on the railroad trains. In 1925, A. Phillip Randolph, a labor and civil rights activist helped organize them into the first black unionized workforce in the nation.

After World War I, manufacturing facilities in the north were beginning to hire a few blacks. These new opportunities ushered in what is known as the Great Migration. The Great Migration represented the largest internal movement of any group in the history of the

United States of America. In droves, nearly six million African Americans left the southern states in search of better treatment and greater opportunities. Two million left the south from 1910 to 1940, during the first period of the Great Migration. Another four million followed in the second period from 1940 thru the 1970's. Migrants left the south in automobiles, buses, and trains. Sometimes people with no mode of transportation hitched rides along the way.

The majority of African Americans that came north from Mississippi and Alabama in the 1920's left the south on the Illinois Central Railroad. The Illinois Central Railroad train brought people from the southern states to places like St. Louis, Missouri and Chicago, Illinois. The last stop was known as the Main Line and it was located at the Illinois Central Depot in Chicago. There, passengers could connect with other rail lines or modes of transportation to get to final destinations like Detroit, Michigan, and Peoria, Illinois.

Train fares were costly and it was hard for many southern sharecroppers to scrape up enough money for the purchase. Even when a person had the ticket fare, they might be prevented by a white clerk from purchasing a ticket to get out of the state. For this reason, it was customary for people to purchase a ticket only to the next train depot where they hoped to find a more sympathetic depot clerk. Those able to pay the fare were allowed to ride in the passenger cars reserved for colored people. Some unable to pay jumped aboard the train's back boxcars and rode like freight. On the Illinois Central Railroad, once the train crossed the Metropolis Bridge African American passengers could get up and change seats. Often the experience was a person's first train ride. Once they arrived in the north, it was the first time many of them mingled among white people.

Fannie Mae's mother Ella (Terrell) Bardley was among the first of Maw Fannie's children to leave Mississippi. She and her younger brother Travis McNeese left the south traveling on the Illinois Central railroad train to Chicago. In 1928, Ella and Travis settled in Peoria, Illinois. The initiative taken by Fannie Mae's mother and uncle led most of their relatives to leave Mississippi during the Great Migration. A phrase they frequently used back then was, "I'm gettin on the next train smokin".

Ella (Terrell) Bardley

After William's mother Rena Clark passed away, he was left with a greater responsibility for assisting his father with his younger siblings. At the same time, William and Fannie Mae wanted children of their own and began to wonder why they hadn't been able to conceive. Eventually, after they were married for almost three years; they were blessed with their first child in October 1932. Their daughter was a beautiful baby girl who they named Ella Mae. Their second child, William Jr. was born three years later in 1935. With the responsibilities of children and making a living for the family, the Clark's found spiritual comfort and solace in their church.

William Clark was a member at St. Peters African Methodist Episcopal Church in Tunica. Fannie Mae was raised in the Baptist Church where her mother Ella Bardley and grandmother, Maw Fannie Brewer were long-time members. As an expression of their spirituality they all enjoyed worshipping God. Fannie Mae would often talk about how as a child her prayer was "God delivery me from the gates of hell".

During a revival meeting at a local Pentecostal church, William and Fannie Mae heard a message that changed their lives. They listened to Evangelist Elder J. H. Price deliver a rousing sermon entitled *Holiness or Hell.* The Clark's were moved spiritually to join the Church of God in Christ founded by Bishop Charles Harrison Mason Sr. They were drawn to the COGIC under the evangelism of Elder J. H. Price in Robinsonville, Mississippi.

Upon joining the COGIC, William and Fannie Mae learned of Bishop Mason's life story. Bishop Charles H. Mason Sr. was the son of slaves, born in Shelby County, Tennessee in 1864. As a youth, Bishop C. H. Mason contracted tuberculosis and yellow fever; both deadly diseases. After the prayers of his mother, siblings, and the local Baptist Church, he was miraculously healed. Bishop Mason believed God healed him and called him to preach. He learned that many Methodist and Baptist church leaders made conversions to a new concept referred to as Holiness and Sanctification. Bishop C. H. Mason began preaching the doctrine in the Baptist Church; and it spread across various states.

Bishop Charles H. Mason Sr. went to Los Angeles, California to investigate the Azusa Street Revival led by Reverend William J.

Seymour in 1907. While there, he experienced the baptism of the Holy Ghost and speaking in unknown tongues. Soon after, he established his own Pentecostal group and was elected the General Overseer. In 1915, Bishop C. H. Mason received the legal rights and charter to name his organization the Church of God in Christ (COGIC). He was Founder and Senior Bishop of the Church of God in Christ in Lexington, Mississippi and in Memphis, Tennessee.

William and Fannie Mae Clark believed wholeheartedly in the COGIC doctrine of Holiness, Sanctification, and the Pentecostal outpouring of the Holy Ghost. The Clark's heard how Bishop Charles H. Mason Sr. fasted, prayed, and was filled with the Holy Spirit. After William and Fannie Mae's diligent prayers, fasting, and supplication they received the Holy Ghost with manifested gifts.

William and Fannie Mae Clark first met Bishop Charles Harrison Mason Sr. at the National Meeting held on Fifth Street in Memphis. When the Fifth Street location was destroyed by fire in 1936, the Clark's began attending on South Lauderdale Street. This was prior to the completion of Mason Temple.

The Clark's enjoyed attending the National Meeting where they witnessed the power of God and saw first-hand how people were miraculously healed and delivered from various infirmities. At that time, living in the segregated south for most black people meant being subjected to Jim Crow laws, substandard living conditions, harsh treatment, and frequent lynching. These horrific conditions resulted in all types of trauma. Many African Americans were suffering from physical and mental afflictions. At church they could receive counsel and moral support from the congregation. People could also shout, dance, or just cry out if they felt the need. The Sanctified church was a place of worship, fellowship and a place where people could release their fears and pain.

Meanwhile, William and Fannie Mae's close relatives continued to leave the south. Most of the cousins Fannie Mae Clark grew up with headed north with their families. Her cousin Riley Parks, Kermit Brooks, and others moved to Flint, Michigan. Her cousin Samuel Parks relocated to Detroit, Michigan. Her cousin Brother Joe May (Famous Gospel Singer) moved to St. Louis, Missouri. Her uncle Lovett Terrell Jr. and her aunts Annie Hughes and Hattie King; who were more of her mother's siblings; all settled in Chicago,

Adelle (Williams) Gordon, Ella Bardley
and Elner Partlow Blackburn

Maw Fannie Brewer was almost sixty years old when her daughter, Elner Partlow Blackburn brought her to Peoria, Illinois.

Fannie Brewer
(Also known as Maw Fannie)

The Yazoo and Mississippi Valley Railroad brought William's family to destinations such as Blytheville, Arkansas and Memphis, Tennessee. William's sister Anna Lee (Clark) Mabry moved to Memphis, Tennessee. William's younger brother, Joseph Clark followed the path of the Southern Railway. He left Mississippi and moved to Plant City, Florida.

The Clark's Aunt Lillie Mae and Uncle Robert Williams left Mississippi in 1936. They moved to Peoria, too. Robert quickly landed a job at a manufacturing plant in the Peoria area. After the good news reached William and Fannie Mae in Robinsonville, they became more determined than ever to leave Mississippi. In early 1937, the Clark's joined their relatives in the Great Migration from the south. William and Fannie Mae were commissioned as Evangelists in the Church of God in Christ. They would spread Bishop Charles H. Mason's COGIC doctrine of Holiness, Sanctification, and the Pentecostal outpouring of the Holy Ghost to the masses of black people in Central Illinois.

Chapter 2.

Family Life, Work and Religion

Family Life, Work, and Religion

William and Fannie Mae Clark arrived in Peoria, Illinois in January of 1937. At that time their daughter Ella Mae was four years old and their son William Jr. was approaching age two. The two children were called by nickname, Sista and Brotha.

The Clark family lived on Paris Road in Peoria Heights. The home was owned by one of Fannie Mae's relatives. For a while Maw Fannie Brewer lived with the family. She eventually married again changing her name to Fannie Brewer Brand. Fannie Mae's mother, Ella Bardley lived in the Paris Road home as well. William and Fannie Mae affectionately called her by nickname Gollie. The Clark children called her Grandmaw. She was loving and very protective and she often spoke on the children's behalf concerning matters. Ella Bardley helped raise the children while her daughter Fannie Mae went to work at her domestic job.

When William Clark first arrived in Peoria, he searched for work all over town. He was not immediately hired anywhere. He continued searching for work in order to provide for his family; which was growing steadily with the birth of their third child Samuel in March of 1937. Refusing to be defeated, William used his own ingenuity to feed his family and make money. As an avid hunter since the earlier days in Mississippi, he knew how to catch rabbits, squirrels and coons which he faithfully brought home to his family, and sold to acquaintances. To make ends meet, William obtained an ice-cream cart from a vending company and he became the local Ice-cream Man.

William and Fannie Mae Clark united with the Church of God in Christ in Peoria under the leadership of Elder S.A. Anderson. The Clark's were both dedicated Evangelists of the COGIC. William was among the roster of Pentecostal Ministers and Fannie Mae was a Missionary. The Clark's lived a Sanctified and upright lifestyle. They followed God's commandments and were very fruitful. They welcomed the birth of their fourth child James in 1938.

Several months before their son, James was born, Nazi Germany and the United States promoted a politically charged boxing match between Heavy-weight Champion Joe Louis and Nazi Germany's boxer, Max Schmeling. Louis defeated Schmeling and the victory was celebrated by millions of Americans, especially black people. Joe Louis's victory shattered supposed Nazi superiority.

World War II began in 1939, after Nazi Germany's invasion of Poland. During that time, President Franklin D. Roosevelt's wife, Eleanor Roosevelt endeared herself to many black people. Many African Americans were inspired by Eleanor Roosevelt. She played a role in establishing the WPA Employment and Infrastructure programs of the depression era. Mother Fannie Mae Clark admired her because she took a public stance against racism. Mrs. Roosevelt invited famous black performer, Marian Anderson to perform at the Lincoln Memorial after she was refused a concert venue. 75,000 people attended the event.

The United States entered World War II in 1941 after Japan attacked Pearl Harbor. Many of the Clark's relatives participated in the war effort. Some voluntarily joined the military. Among them were Travis McNeese who joined the U.S. Army; and Riley Parks Jr. joined the U.S Air Force. Black people were hired to work in large manufacturing plants producing all types of equipment supporting the war. In 1941, William Clark was hired by Caterpillar Tractor Company in East Peoria, Illinois. He was among the first black men hired by the company.

Before William Clark left for work in the morning, Fannie Mae was sure to pack his toolbox-sized lunchbox with his favorite foods. Fannie Mae would prepare a large thermos of coffee to satisfy his frequent request "Coffee Me". When William brought his pay check home from Caterpillar, he would give it right away to his wife. Usually, twenty dollars was reserved for his personal use. Fannie Mae used the remainder of his paycheck for the family expenses.

Fannie Mae Clark knew how to shop for bargain items at five and dimes, and with her friends and church community. Many of the women of the church canned fresh fruits. They sold jars of canned fruit preserves. Strawberry, apricot, and peach were favorite flavors. Some people sold fresh caught fish and fresh raised chickens. Others sold bags of fresh nuts, like pecans, walnuts, and peanuts. Sometimes people pushed carts full of fresh fruits and vegetables. A staple item purchased for the Clark household was a fifty pound bag of potatoes. The Clark's appreciated the benefit of potatoes because they could fill an empty stomach well. They prepared potatoes various ways. Deep fried seasoned potatoes were a well-loved tradition that the Clark family simply referred to as Tadus.

William and Fannie Mae Clark were loving parents who were uniquely qualified for the task of rearing children. They would be blessed by God with seventeen children over three decades.

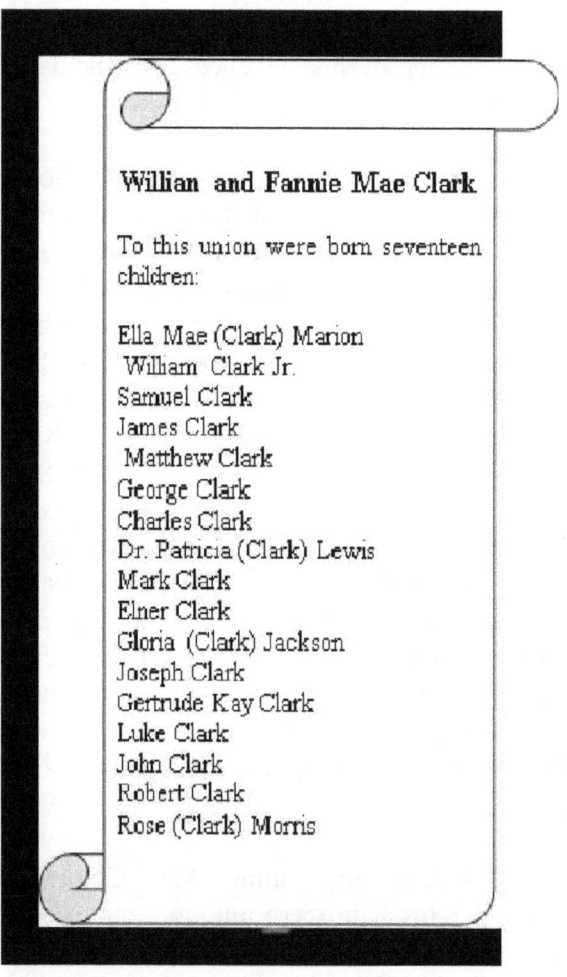

Willian and Fannie Mae Clark

To this union were born seventeen children:

Ella Mae (Clark) Marion
William Clark Jr.
Samuel Clark
James Clark
Matthew Clark
George Clark
Charles Clark
Dr. Patricia (Clark) Lewis
Mark Clark
Elner Clark
Gloria (Clark) Jackson
Joseph Clark
Gertrude Kay Clark
Luke Clark
John Clark
Robert Clark
Rose (Clark) Morris

Missionary Fannie Mae Clark

Elder William Clark Sr.

In 1946, William Clark Sr. was appointed Elder Pastor of Lincoln Avenue

Church of God in Christ, in Peoria, Illinois. The church was a two-story storefront building located at 1013 West Lincoln Avenue. The church members converted the downstairs into a Sanctuary for praise and worship. The Sanctified community throughout the area gathered to fellowship there. Elder Clark and Mother Clark worked diligently with the membership at Lincoln Avenue COGIC to carry out ministry and missions. Church services were held regularly on weekdays, usually Tuesdays and Fridays; and twice on Sunday. There were services for Praise and Worship, Prayer and Consecration, Revivals, Shut-ins, Healing of the Sick, Save and Deliverance, and Tarry Services for the Holy Ghost. Each service began promptly with prayer, bible verses, and devotional congregational songs.

Mark Clark was born at Saint Francis Hospital in Peoria, Illinois on June 28, 1947. He became a member of Lincoln Avenue COGIC by birthright. Mark's birth occurred one year after his father became an Elder Pastor, assuring he would receive a thorough education in religious principles, practices, and doctrine. Mark carried the distinction of being Elder William and Fannie Mae Clark's seventh son; signaling his extraordinary life path. He was the ninth of their seventeen children and his unique birth order would allow him to develop a heightened awareness of injustice.

Mark and his siblings began observing their parents as they carried out church ministry and work. As a child, Mark would listen attentively to his father's Pentecostal preaching and teaching. The entire church congregation took notice of Elder Clark's reverent mannerisms as he entered the Church Sanctuary. He made sure to kneel down in prayer before taking a seat in the ministerial pulpit. Mark would watch as his father delivered the word of God with zeal and determination. When Elder Clark preached, he preached hard and with all his power and might. He would place his hands on his ear, as if to show that he was receiving the word directly from God at that moment. Through call and response, he had a keen ability to engage the congregation and his church members participated fully in his sermons.

As an ordained Elder Pastor of the Church of God in Christ, the vestments Mark's father wore on ceremonial occasions consisted of a long black robe with a white collar. The Pastoral Cross was suspended around his neck by a black cord. On his head, he wore a black Kufi beanie symbolic of his status as a spiritual leader and wise elder. He showed pride in his African heritage and culture. On his feet he wore black silk socks and black Stacey Adams shoes; which he enlisted one of his sons to shine from heel to toe. On Sundays, he wore a black suit with a white starched shirt and black tie.

Elder William Clark Sr.

Mother Clark normally wore suits and dresses fashioned long enough in length so that her hemline was well below her knees. She often accompanied her clothing with a matching hat. On special occasions she wore white, symbolic of the Holiness of the Saints. The Clark girls wore dresses, or skirts and blouses to church services. On special occasions such as Easter Sunday, they wore more elaborate dresses and accessorized with purses, gloves, and dress shoes. The boys usually wore suits and ties or white shirts and dark colored pants. Usually the boys hurried to take off their dressy church clothes as soon as they left the church building.

Mark and his siblings were active in the Lincoln Avenue Sunday school program during their formative years. The program was designed to improve biblical knowledge and teach principles and good character. The Sunday School teachers took the children through a process of classroom discussion and congregational review. The children were given small picture cards containing bible characters and verses to read and discuss with the class. At the end of each lesson, the children reviewed what they learned with the entire congregation.

Mother Fannie Mae Clark was a Poet. She told the children bible stories designed to teach lessons and motivate them to improve behavior. Her stories entertained the children and reinforced spiritual principles and values. Next to God and Jesus, her favorite character in the bible was most definitely David; and she enjoyed telling the children bible stories about his various exploits.

Mother Clark talked about how David slew the giant, Goliath. Whenever she told the story she reminded the children, saying, "If you have the favor of God, you can slew a giant, no matter how big it is, all you need is a rock and sling". She told the children about how David was pursued by an evil King who controlled a nation, and how God turned his situation around and made him King. She would get excited whenever she talked about what David did; and especially when she talked about how he praise danced and played the tambourine. Whenever she talked about David's dancing, she would begin to dance. Sometimes she would say ""Hey, I want to dance like David danced"! Mother Clark would dance as if she were King David, but just for a little while. Once she stopped, she always commented, saying "That's why God favored David, because he loved to praise God with the music and dance".

Mark Clark listened attentively as his mother told bible stories. As a child, he learned lessons of defeating enemies, establishing kingdoms, and trampling down evil with courage, determination, and by the power of God. Mother Clark was full of wisdom and knowledge and she inspired her children to exhibit courage, determination, and the better human qualities and characteristics.

Elder William and Fannie Mae Clark were the most influential people in Mark Clark's life. They led lives that were excellent examples of family, faith, and community. Although Mark and his siblings referred to their parents at home as Momma and Daddy, during church or when speaking more formally, they were addressed by religious titles as Elder Clark and Mother Clark. They made sure the children attended church regularly and participated in church functions like the choir, Sunshine Band, Sunday School, and Young People Willing Workers (YPWW) to promote their spiritual growth and build character.

Mother Clark enjoyed picking up special little items at the local thrift stores that she would distribute to the children. She made sure they had plenty of goodies and snacks. Sometimes she made elaborate sweets and treats like gingerbread houses or jelly bean trees. They were almost too beautiful to eat at first but so inviting that no trace of them remained before long. She enjoyed entertaining the children too. Sometimes she would put the smaller ones on her knee, while rocking them gently, singing her family-famous song "Go Down Town and Get Some Candy".

Mark's mother was an excellent cook. She incorporated many of the old southern traditions. She made delicious southern fried chicken, turkey and dressing, and what she called "beef stenographer" because it was similar to beef stroganoff. Usually, Mother Clark prepared huge meals to ensure that her large household were properly fed. Her specialty was baking cakes and pies. She made sweet potatoes pies, pecan pies, coconut cream pies, peach cobblers, chocolate cakes, yellow cakes, cupcakes, wedding cakes, birthday cakes, and cakes for no occasion at all. Mother Clark was a professional cake decorator who would often prepare them for her friends and church community.

Mother Clark played many roles in the church and the entire congregation gravitated to her. They especially enjoyed hearing her recite poetry because of her determined voice, facial expressions, and hand motions that kept the audience amused and entertained. Among Mother Clark's favorite recitals were *When the Devil Goes to Church* and *Jonah and the Whale*. The church congregation would give her rousing applause whenever she delivered poetry. They would frequently request that she recite another of her favorite poems.

Mother Clark was the Senior Choir Conductor. It was her responsibility to keep the older choir members on beat with the music. It was a role that she didn't take lightly; and one that she thoroughly enjoyed. She had no formal training as a Choir Conductor and was not specifically musically inclined; but she was dedicated to the job. She went to a music store where she purchased an orchestra baton and a book, *How to become an Orchestra Conductor*. The book showed specific motions one could make using their orchestra baton. One of the easiest baton movements to learn was the horizontal figure-eight motion. At home, Mother Clark practiced choir conducting by waiving her orchestra baton. It brought plenty of smiles to the children's faces while watching. As the children watched, she would attempt more elaborate motions that she picked up from watching other choir conductors. During church services, she kept it simple. She made the horizontal figure-eight motions back and forth during nearly every song. It was quite amusing to watch Mother Clark conduct the Senior Choir using her orchestra baton. Her dedication to the role, and her motions and mannerism brought the church congregation alive with lots of smiles; and it helped the Senior Choir members stay on beat.

Chapter 3.

Servant Leadership and Elementary Education

Servant Leadership and Elementary Education

Elder William Clark, Sr.

Motto of Servant Leadership: St .John 9:4 " I must work the works of him that sent me, while it is day: for when night cometh, no man can work".

Mark Clark's father was a servant of the people. During the early 1950's, Elder William Clark and several of his trusted church members traveled into Tunica County, Mississippi to pick up people who were unable to leave. Some had no money or means of transportation. Others owed debts to white people and were prevented from leaving town on public transportation. Blacks in Tunica lived in total segregation. They were subjected to Jim Crow laws and harsh treatment. Many men, women, and children were lynched in Tunica; and among the victims was Fannie Mae Clark's uncle. Tunica, Mississippi was the poorest city in the nation. Some blacks lived in a part of Tunica known as Sugar Ditch Alley. The houses had no indoor plumbing and people used an open sewer out in back the houses, which they called Sugar Ditch. The houses along its banks were dilapidated and infested with all kinds of vermin.

Elder William Clark Sr. and his group of Ministers and Deacons at Lincoln Avenue COGIC brought people out of Tunica, Mississippi by automobile caravan. Traveling by caravan, they could watch out for one another as they traveled through the segregated south. Elder Clark kept a copy of the Green Book in case of an emergency. He used it to direct him to safe locations where black people were welcome. The caravan traveled by night and usually arrived in Peoria, Illinois by morning.

Mark Clark was a young boy when his father and the Lincoln Avenue COGIC members traveled back and forth to Tunica, Mississippi. Older brother, Matthew Clark described how their father brought people back to Peoria. Some migrants were housed in the Lincoln Avenue church until they were placed with a member in the COGIC congregation. Matthew talked about how impressed he was to see their father's heroism and how many in the congregation came from Mississippi.

Elder Clark was a servant leader who worked along-side dedicated church members. They participated in all types of functions at the church; and they headed various departments and auxiliaries. Among the roster of Ministers were Assistant Pastor, Omie Taylor, Elder Felton Beck Sr., Minister Chester Warr, Minister Willie Artis and Elder Monroe Williams. Among the trusted church Deacons were Brother James Littles, and Brother Isaiah Danage.

Men of Lincoln Avenue Church of God in Christ
Front row: Brother Chatman, Elder Pastor William Clark Sr. and Brother Williams.
Back row: Assistant Pastor, Omie Taylor, Brother White, Brother Troop, Brother Boddie, Brother Robert, Brother Isaiah Danage, and Brother Robinson.

Women of Lincoln Avenue Church of God in Christ
Front Row: Mother Julia Boddie, Mother Bessie Taylor, Mother Margaret Williams, Mother Powell and Mother Watson. In Back row: Sister Morgan, Mother Fannie Mae Clark, Mother Littles, Sister Carroll, Mother Russell and Mother Williams.

Mother Green was over the Sunshine Band. Her role was to support each of the children's spiritual growth and development. As a child, Mark Clark traveled with her and the Lincoln Avenue COGIC Sunshine Band to the

State Holy Convocation in Chicago, Illinois. All the children loved Mother Green. She worked on building their character, faith, and self-worth. Under her tutelage, the children participated in all types of activities to improve knowledge of the bible, and strengthen values.

The Lincoln Avenue
Church of God in Christ
Sunshine Band

The Lincoln Avenue Church of God in Christ congregation in Peoria, Illinois.

Lincoln Avenue Church of God in Christ was a place where people went to reach out to one another in fellowship. The church members held testimony service where people talked about how God watched over them. Some in the congregation told lengthy stories of dealing with adversities and battling the devil. Others proclaimed how God delivered them. Mother Clark encouraged the children to participate in testimony service. She would remind them not to be ashamed of standing up and telling others of God's goodness. For this reason, Mark and the other children stood and said a brief and simplistic testimony. They usually gave honor to God, the Pastor, the church Elders and Mothers, and they thanked God for waking them up in the morning.

The Lincoln Avenue church had a small kitchen and dining space upstairs where congregants could sit down and eat. The women of the church, some in white uniforms and comfortable white shoes prepared scrumptious meals for the congregation. They usually made chicken dinners, dressing, greens, and cornbread which they served after special church services. Mother Riley prepared meals for the congregation most Sundays, and she was an excellent cook. Sometimes the smell of her creations would seep up through the walls and permeate throughout the church building.

At church, the Elders, Ministers, Missionaries, and Evangelists held Tarry Services to usher in the Holy Ghost. The Elder Ministers would lay their hands on the heads of congregants while praying and anointing their head with Holy ointment. The Ministers and Mothers would prompt the congregants to receive the Holy Spirit. They would speak in their ears words like, "Let the Lord have his way", "Tell the Lord Thank You", and "Call on the Lord". White sheets were used to throw over those who fell down slain in the Spirit. The white sheets symbolized Holiness and protected modesty.

The congregation at Lincoln Avenue Church of God in Christ engaged in rhythmic and poly-rhythmic hand-clapping and double-clapping sessions during church services. This helped the congregation get into a more spiritual zone. The hand-clapping, holy dancing, tarrying, and spirit baptism were all powerful displays of COGIC worship. These were expressions of spirituality with many of the elements based on West African tradition.

Music was very important to the church. The church members sung congregational songs and enjoyed hearing selections from local singers and the church choir. Elder Clark made sure their children participated. The Clark's encouraged their children to take piano lessons. They organized the four youngest children into a Clark Quartet. Mother Clark loved to hear and sing devotional songs. Among her favorites were *Jesus I'll Never Forget What You Done For Me*, and *I'm So Glad Jesus Lifted Me*. Hearing devotional songs and uplifting songs accompanied by skilled musicians on instruments like piano, drums, organ, and electric guitar helped to emphasize that a mighty move of God was taking place. In the Sanctified tradition, the music prompted shouting, hand-clapping, dancing, and tarrying for the Holy Ghost.

On special occasions, the church would host Musicals where more well-known singers appeared before the congregation. The day Brother Joe May performed was one such occasion that electrified the entire church community. Brother Joe May was Mother

Fannie Mae Clark's first cousin; and he was one of the greatest male soloists in the history of gospel music. He was known as "The Thunderbolt of the Mid-West". The response was overwhelming when the COGIC in Illinois heard that Brother Joe May would be performing at Lincoln Avenue. To accommodate the large crowd size, the event was moved to the lawn at the Carver Community Center. It was a big deal, and thousands of people attended the event. Brother Joe May sung many well-loved gospel songs including his version of one of the most popular songs of that time; *Move On Up A Little Higher*. For many years, the COGIC throughout the State of Illinois talked about the day that Brother Joe May came.

Elder William Clark's sister, Irene (Clark) Howard was President of the Lincoln Avenue Usher Board and Vice-President of the Adult Choir. She followed her brother to Peoria and worked diligently in the church. In 1952, Irene and her husband Frank Howard suffered a devastating loss when their seven children perished in a house fire. The pain and trauma of their experience was almost unbearable. The Clark's and the Lincoln Avenue COGIC congregation did what they could to help the couple make it through. Eventually, their pain would subside and they would be blessed by God with seven more children. The loss they suffered would never be forgotten.

By the early 1950's, the Clark's oldest daughter, Ella Mae was a young woman. She was considered one of the most beautiful girls in Peoria, Illinois. Her beauty caught the eye of many men who wanted to marry her. The Clark's wanted her to marry one of the Deacons at the church. She wanted to experience life so she moved to St. Louis, Missouri as soon as she could. While in St. Louis, she married and gave birth to her first child, Daryl.

By the mid-1950's, the Clark family moved from Peoria Heights into the inner-city near downtown. The Clark's home was on First Street between McArthur Highway and South Sheridan Road (now North Richard Pryor Place). The First Street home was a simple wood-framed two-story house which was probably originally constructed in the 1920's. The house was across from the Historic St. Joseph's Catholic Church. As the Clark's left home on Sunday mornings headed for Lincoln Avenue they would notice the white people gathered for Sunday services at St. Joseph's. Sometimes during the weekdays the Clark children would go across the street and sit on the front steps of the Catholic Church. They admired the architectural work and the church's large steeple from where the church bell rung daily.

The corner at First Street and South Sheridan

On the corner of First Street and South Sheridan Road, directly across from the church was Dentino Brothers store. The children made frequent trips to the storefront grocery stores on each corner of the block. They usually purchased candy or picked up items for their mother on her grocery store account. Mother Clark often reminded the children about the times before Elder Clark began working at Caterpillar Tractor Company. During those times food was scarce, money was really tight, and the storefront grocery stores help people make it through hard times.

Mother Clark recalled times when it appeared the family might miss an evening meal. She and Elder Clark operated in faith and walked in confidence that God would supply the family's needs. She prayed about their food situation before she went to work at her domestic job. When she left from work that evening, she passed by a building where she heard a man say "Come over here and take a look at these greens". When she heard it, she waived him off and quickly said in a low tone of voice "I don't have any money". Then the man responded, "I didn't ask you if you had any money, I asked you to take a look at these greens. Mother Clark stopped, went over and looked at the greens. Immediately, she thought in her mind that she wished she could purchase them for her family but she didn't say a word. Then he said to her, "I tell you what, I'm going to give you these greens and all these fixings to go with it; and all you have to do is promise me that you will shop at my local grocery store because I'm new in town". That night, Mother Clark brought home greens, corn meal, flour, sugar, milk, eggs, meat, and all types of food. The Clark's had a fine meal and they were able to pick up groceries anytime they needed them on their new grocery store account. Whenever Mother Clark recalled that experience, she quoted David from the book of Psalms saying "I have been young, and now I am old, yet never have I seen the righteous forsaken, nor his seed begging bread".

During holidays and special occasions almost every inch of physical space in the Clark home was taken up by a member of the family, or a close relative, or a friend. Although the home was equipped with several bedrooms upstairs and down, there was limited space because of the numerous children and extended family members that frequented there. The love and respect for one another, the hospitality toward guests, and Elder and Mother Clark's sponsored dinners helped forge bonds that linked them together in a special way. Mark Clark's bond with his parents and the entire family was strong.

In 1955, Mark Clark was eight years old. That year Emmett Till, a teenager from Illinois was murdered by racist white men. He was visiting relatives in Mississippi at the time. His mother, Mamie Till Bradley (later known as Mamie Till-Mobley) held an open casket funeral urging the world to look at the racial injustice that had been done to her son. Emmett Till had been beaten, disfigured, shot in the head, and dumped in a river. His funeral was held in Chicago, Illinois at the Historic Roberts Temple Church of God in Christ where service was officiated by Reverend Isaiah Roberts. Bishop Louis Henry Ford, Presiding Prelate of the Historic Illinois First Jurisdiction of the COGIC gave the eulogy.

The murder of Emmett Till taught young Mark about the racial tensions and brutality occurring across the nation. It showed him just how turbulent times were and how many African Americans were routinely victimized

Mark saw the great outpouring of sadness and grief on the faces of his parents and siblings. Observing how the brutal death affected the community, he experienced the collective nightmare of African Americans all across the nation. During that pivotal time in history, many activists and religious leaders began to speak out against racism and injustice. Mark would observe the rise of activism growing up in Peoria, Illinois.

In 1955, Bishop Charles H. Mason Sr. appointed Pastor Eleazar Lenox, Bishop of the Southern Illinois Ecclesiastical Jurisdiction of the COGIC. Bishop E. Lenox was Founder of Greater Holy Temple COGIC in Chicago, Illinois. He appointed Mark Clark's father to serve as Superintendent of Greater Central Illinois District of the COGIC. Elder William Clark Sr. would travel throughout Central Illinois assisting congregations extending from Peoria, Kewanee, Jacksonville, and Springfield, Illinois. During that time, the Civil Rights Movement was beginning to pick up steam. In December of that year, the Montgomery Bus Boycott began. It was inspired by the actions of Rosa Parks and led by Reverend Dr. Martin Luther King, Jr., President of the Southern Christian Leadership Conference (SCLC).

By the time the Montgomery Bus Boycott was over, the Clark's five oldest sons were registered for the Military Selective Service Draft. Several of the Clark brothers enlisted in the military voluntarily, entering on a buddy system. As young adults, it was time for William Jr., Samuel, James, Matthew, and George to move out from under the strict disciplinary code of their parents. They were given essentially two choices; military or college. All five of the Clark brothers went to the U.S. Army. When military officials discovered that Matthew did not meet the age requirements for induction, he was released. James was released from the military as well.

Mark Clark's grandmother, Ella Bardley eventually moved out of the Clark's home into her own apartment in the Warner Homes Public Housing Project. It was a couple of blocks away from the Clark's house. Constantly, the children would visit her to enjoy the loving warmth of her presence. She was a woman who showed genuine concern for everyone and she made sure her neighbors at her apartment building had a decent meal. One of Ella Bardley's neighbors was a man called by the name Lieutenant. He suffered from severe alcoholism and was known for falling asleep in the stairwell of the apartment building. She was not the type of person who would watch Lieutenant lying there and keep on going. She would go over and fuss at him saying, "Lieutenant, you get on up from here". She would continue to fuss at him until he headed toward his own apartment. Sometimes, she recruited her grandsons to go check on him. When Lieutenant was too inebriated to walk, the Clark boys assisted with the task of getting him to the safety of his apartment.

Mark Clark learned lots of lessons growing up in his large household with his numerous siblings and relatives. His closest brother in age was Charles; and he was three years older. He would educate his younger brother throughout their growing years. Elner Clark was one year younger than Mark; and Patricia was one year older. She recalled an incident she would never forget. It occurred when Mark was about ten or eleven years old.

Older brother George gave Mark strict instructions not to ride his bicycle which was in disrepair with only half of its handlebars functional. Refusing to let that stop him, he brought the bicycle out after George left home.

Mark Clark at ten (10) years old.

Mark and Patricia took turns riding George's bicycle. After a while, they decided that two people could ride at one time; so she paddled and steered while he sat on the handlebars. During their ride, he kept wiggling on the broken handlebars. Eventually, the bike tipped over. They both fell off but Patricia was injured in the fall. The handlebar scraped her leg creating a big gash.

Mark pushed the bicycle back home with Patricia limping and bleeding from her knee. When they arrived home, their father took her to the hospital to get stitched up. Mark felt bad about his sister's injury; and about riding his brother's bike without permission. That day, he repeatedly checked on his sister and told her how sorry he was. Mark was the type of person that admitted his mistakes and apologized for his wrong actions. He made it a point to go talk to George about what happened. Mark admitted to his brother that he should have listened. George was angry at first but after a short while he was distributing sugar cookies to Mark and the rest of his younger siblings like he always did.

Mark and several of his siblings walked to Lincoln Elementary School together. The School didn't serve breakfast or lunch so the children had to walk home to eat. When the children arrived home for lunch, their mother or grandmother had lunch already prepared. Usually, lunch consisted of potatoes and a hamburger for nourishment with a glass of Kool-Aid to quench their thirst. Once the children finished lunch, they would hurry back to Lincoln Elementary School to complete the remainder of their school day.

Mark Clark attended Lincoln Elementary School in Peoria, Illinois.

Mark's birth order in the Clark family, with eight older siblings and eight younger siblings; uniquely positioned him to develop a keen awareness of injustice early in life. He was more fortunate than many children who came to school hungry most mornings or who had nothing to eat during lunch-time. He believed in looking out for the less fortunate and sharing what he had. He often invited friends over during lunch-time just to ensure that they ate a decent meal.

The Clark children would sometimes accompany their parents to the International Holy Convocation in Memphis. Normally, the girls went and the older boys stayed home. In 1958, Mark stayed home with his older brothers while Patricia was among the children that attended. She participated in most church activities and attended the Convocation regularly.

Elder Clark sometimes met with Bishop Mason and other COGIC leaders while visiting Mason Temple. On one occasion he was leaving a meeting with the Bishop, when he noticed his daughter standing in the corridor. Elder Clark quickly brought her into the meeting room and introduced her. Bishop Charles H. Mason greeted her in a friendly manner, gently shaking her hand. At first, Patricia noticed his small stature. The Bishop was not much taller than she was; yet she knew of his ministry and she felt the awesome power of his spiritual presence. It was a great honor for her to meet the Founder of the Church of God in Christ. Patricia was twelve years old when she met the Founder of the COGIC, Bishop Charles H. Mason Sr.

As Mark Clark began approaching his teenage years, he began spending more time with his older brothers. He would listen as James, Matthew, and Charles engaged in debates about religion, politics, and whether the system would ever work justly for black people. Mark's brothers discussed colonialism and the plight of black people all over the world. The brutal death of Emmet Till and the frequent incidents of racial injustice occurring throughout the country deeply concerned them. They would help educate their brother about what was happening in the world.

Mark's older brothers, William Jr., Samuel, and George were on active duty in the military. They were stationed in Germany together for a period of time. William Jr was a U.S. Army Infantryman. He would serve a combined twelve years during the Korean War, and the Vietnam War. Samuel served in the U.S. Army's Tank Battalion. He completed his tour of duty in the U.S. Army in the late 1950's. George was a Military Policeman. He would serve two tours of duty. William Jr. and George would not complete their tours in the military for several years. When they return from the wars in Indochina, they would assist with the task of preparing their younger brother for the struggle.

Chapter 4.

Mark's Early Teens - An Introduction to Activism

Mark's Early Teens – An Introduction to Activism

In 1960, Mark Clark's older siblings returned home to visit family in Peoria. Whenever the older Clark siblings came home, they gathered the family together and shared their experiences. While they conversed with one another, they updated each other on various conflicts that were going on in the world, including the wars in Indochina. William Jr. shared stories about the Korean War and how he and other soldiers survived by digging trenches. He talked about how the U.S. made little progress after China's involvement in the conflict. Samuel talked about the DMZ, and how the tanks carried out the various armored maneuvers and artillery bombardments. George shared stories about his patrol duties as a Military Policeman.

The Clark's oldest daughter Ella Mae (Clark) Marion returned from St. Louis, Missouri. When she arrived in Peoria, she was dressed in the finest clothing and wearing Stone Marten. Her son, Daryl wore a camel-colored Cashmere coat with a matching Cashmere hat.

Ella Mae was stylish, classy, and extremely beautiful. Many men watched her as she sashayed down the street. Several men damaged their vehicles on Sheridan Road because they were fixated on her beauty.

Ella Mae (Clark) Marion
(Also known as Sista)

William Clark Jr.
(Also known as Brotha)

Fourteen of the seventeen Clark children. Back row: William Jr., Ella Mae, George, Charles, Matthew, Patricia, Samuel. Middle row: Joseph, Gloria, and Elner. Front row: Grandson Daryl, John, Luke, Mother Fannie Mae Clark holding Rose, Elder William Clark Sr. and Kay.

While the Clark's children were all in town, Mother Clark wanted a photograph of her large family. She enlisted a part-time photographer, who also happened to be her home repairman. The photo was planned to be taken immediately after Sunday morning church services but it kept being postponed for several hours. It was always difficult to get the Clark family in a room together at the same time. The Sunday afternoon when the home repairman took the family photograph was no exception. When one child came in it seemed as if another one left. After almost four hours of waiting, Elder Clark told the home repairman to go ahead and take the photo. When the photo was finally taken, three of the Clark siblings were not in it. Older sibling James was nowhere to be found. Younger sibling Robert was sleeping. Mark, who was camera shy; went outside avoiding the family portrait.

Ella Mae eventually moved to a small apartment nearby. The proximity was so close that the family could frequently visit one another. At her apartment, they could listen to the latest soul music on the radio while avoiding the strict oversight of home. They listen to popular songs like *The Twist* by Chubby Checker and *Stand by Me* by Ben E. King. Ella Mae would play her favorite albums on her record player. She enjoyed dancing to the latest tunes and smoking Lucky Strikes cigarettes. She also loved talking about the "Say Hey Kid", famous Major League Baseball player, Willie Mays.

During the holidays, Ella Mae was known for making Turkey Hash. She was an excellent cook, following in her mother's and grandmother's footsteps. When she attended family gatherings, someone was sure to inquire about when she might make the dish next. She would make good use of all the leftover turkey, potatoes, and other vegetables; seasoning them with herbs and spices. Sometimes she served Turkey Hash over biscuits which made it a hearty and delicious meal that could satisfy a large gathering. Eventually, it became a tradition in the Clark family to make Turkey Hash after a holiday.

By the early 1960's, the Clark's older children; Ella Mae, William Jr., Samuel, James, Matthew, and George were adults beginning their own families. Elder Clark and Mother Clark stood proudly at several of their children's wedding ceremonies. They became loving grandparents as their children had offspring. The Clark's ancestral branches were beginning their own extensions; and times were certainly changing!

Parents of the bride (left); and Mother Fannie Mae Clark and Elder William Clark Sr.
Back Row: Samuel Clark

The 1960's was a transitional period for the Church of God in Christ. In 1961, COGIC Founder, Bishop Charles H. Mason passed away at 95 years old. Members of the Church of God in Christ and the religious community around the world grieved his loss. The Clark family was among those who mourned the loss of the great spiritual leader. Elder William Clark Sr. traveled to Memphis, Tennessee, and he attended Bishop Mason's Home Going Services at Mason Temple. Bishop Ozro T. Jones, Sr. gave the Home Going eulogy. Afterwards, Bishop Charles Harrison Mason Sr. was entombed in the memorial wing of Mason Temple Church of God in Christ.

During Bishop Mason's lifetime, he was known to be a supporter of equal rights but he kept the COGIC organization's main focus on saving souls. In the early days of the Civil Rights Movement, the COGIC organization did not openly sanction its members to engage in protests, boycotts, and demonstrations. These were felt by many as not setting a Godly tone and being too confrontational. For this reason, some claimed the COGIC was an apolitical religious organization with limited involvement in the movement.

During the early days of the Civil Rights Movement, the Black Church; mainly African Methodist, Baptist, and the Nation of Islam were coordinating with activists and nationalist organizations like the Student Nonviolent Coordination Committee (SNCC), Congress of Racial Equality (CORE), National Association for the Advancement of Colored People (NAACP), and Southern Christian Leadership Conference (SCLC). Their combined efforts led to greater success in achieving demands. As the movement shifted its focus from ending segregation to economic empowerment, jobs and housing in the 1960's, the Church of God in Christ organization and its members would increase their active participation

Meanwhile, in the early 1960's, the Clark family moved from their First Street house into a home located on Seventh Street. The new house had a more up-to-date kitchen and a much larger dining area. When the Clark's entertained visiting church members and extended family, the living room could be partitioned off for greater privacy. Bedrooms and bathrooms were downstairs and the upstairs was large enough to accommodate several more beds for the numerous Clark boys.

The back porch of the Seventh Street home was where the Clark family congregated throughout the summer months. While the older siblings sat and talked, they watched over the younger siblings. The girls played hop-scotch and jumped rope. The older boys gave instructions to the younger boys while they constantly repaired bicycle parts and patched inner-tubes in the back yard. Nearby, there was a small uncapped well in the ground which appeared as if it had long since dried up. The children found it useful for pitching old tokens and a few pennies. Mark practiced his pitching skills there.

Elder Clark parked the family's automobile in the garage near the back alley. Among the vehicles owned over the years was a Buick Electra 225, known as the Deuce and a Quarter. He drove it to work, church, and on frequent out of town trips. Each Friday, he drove Mother Clark and the children shopping. They normally went to grocery stores and general merchandise stores. On Saturday mornings he often drove them to the hairdresser's house. She was a member of the church; who pressed and curled hair with a hot comb and styled it. There were many talented entrepreneurs in the community; and the Clark's utilized their products, skills and abilities.

Several of the women at the church were seamstresses. Mother Clark would commission them to create her a beautiful suit or dress. Elder Clark would drive her to fittings and to pick up the garment as soon as it was finished. The Clark's made sure to support black entrepreneurs. People would come by the house selling items like herbal remedies, rubs and ointments to help relieve aches and pains. Products such as ointments, soaps, candles, clothing, and numerous volumes of encyclopedias were all purchased from people that they knew in the community or who came by the house. On weekends, the home repairman usually came over to repair broken fixtures. The life insurance man came by to collect the monthly premium. Both the home repairman and life insurance man were relatives of church members.

Periodically, the family drove to pick up fast food. A favorite spot was Big-Johns Barbeque, a well-known black owned business in Peoria. Sometimes the family went to Sandys for Burgers or Velvet Freeze to purchase Coney Dogs. Among the family's favorite fast food item was Tenderloin sandwiches. They were sold at restaurants all around town. No other city made Tenderloin sandwiches like in Peoria.

Rose Clark
(The Clark's seventeenth child)

Elder Clark drove the family downtown Peoria to shop at department stores, and to Sheridan Village Shopping Center, too. When Mother Clark couldn't find what she wanted in the stores or local community, she would order items out of her Montgomery Ward's Catalog. All types of items would arrive in the mail that Mother Clark ordered for the family.

On occasion, Elder Clark drove the family on joy rides. He usually rode across one of the bridges toward East Peoria and then went back home. During the Christmas holiday, he drove the family downtown to look at all the décor and lights. He drove out by War Memorial Drive to look at the homes where the more well-to-do white people lived. The family would observe how illuminated many of the homes were. The Clark's did not particularly care for bringing a Christmas tree or lights into their own home. They celebrated their belief in the birth of Christ, not Saturnalia.

When the Clark family went on summer outings, they went to Glen Oak Park and Detwieller Park to spend quality time together. They would roast weenies, eat watermelon, enjoy nature, and let the children run around. Elder Clark was a good athlete in his earlier days and he still enjoyed foot racing. Just to remind the family of his capabilities, he would challenge one or two of his sons in a foot race. Elder Clark would give his sons a running head-start but somehow he always caught up to them and passed them by. It provided the family with lots of laughter to see him racing his sons; and it let the entire family know just how fast he was.

Elder Clark and Mother Clark had a traditional old-school style marriage. They both worked together for the betterment of their large family. Mother Clark worked as Cook at Saint Francis Hospital for a period of time. She was responsible for preparing the hospital's breakfast. Her specialty item was making all the bacon strips. She also performed domestic work for a prominent Peoria attorney and physician.

Elder Clark kept a close eye on the family and he monitored the children's activities. The Clark children usually fared best when following two rules; the first rule was that children stayed out of grown folk's business; and the second rule was similar to the first, that they stay in a child's place. The Clark's refused to let the children attend dances, movie theaters, or drive-ins. They only wanted them to listen to gospel music. If they heard any of their children listening to Soul, Blues, Jazz, or whatever else on the radio; they would say "Turn Off That Blues". Elder Clark made sure that Mark and everyone else in his household were following rules.

Elder Clark was head of the household and received the utmost respect from the family. When he gave an order, it was adhered to without sluggishness because the children all knew he meant business. He was a strict disciplinarian. He felt strongly about the children behaving appropriately, both inside and outside the home. He was observant, listening attentively to conversation; ensuring the children were communicating respectfully. He made sure the children utilized good manners and were saying "Yes Sir" and "Yes Ma'am" when responding to their parents or other adults. Elder Clark monitored the children's non-verbal expressions and eye movements for any inch of rebelliousness. He was known to take off his thick leather belt "The Strap"; which he used to thwart even perceived disobedience.

When Elder Clark came home, the sound was as if thunder rolled. There was a loud sound of children's footsteps scrambling as he approached. The children knew that they better grab a broom or a wipe cloth and position themselves in a work-like posture. Elder Clark would inspect the house for cleanliness as soon as he came in. He was especially particular about any paper on the floor. If he observed a small piece of paper, he would point to it and say, "Pick up them giblets of paper". Sometimes Elder Clark's stern directives and pointing would make one or two of the children so nervous that it temporarily blinded them. Out of fear, the children were not always able to see a little giblet of paper right in front of their face.

The Clark's made sure their children were participating in wholesome activities like music classes, art, theatrical plays, and spelling bees. They approved of the children going to the local library, engaging in youth activities at Carver Community Center, swimming at Proctor Recreation Center, and attending an occasional baseball game. The children were encouraged to participate in enrichment programs and attend youth camps. Mark was involved in many of these activities during his youth.

During Mark's early teenage years, he developed into an observant and intelligent young man. He began sharing his thoughts and insights; often questioning the status quo. While attending Roosevelt Junior High School, he was accused of a violent outburst and fighting after he confronted a white teacher for making disparaging remarks. Mark was expelled from school and sent to a Juvenile Detention Center. He returned to school the following semester and would later go on to Manual High School. The Peoria school system's bias education and disparate treatment would create an environment where his inquisitive mind would rarely be inspired. The failures of the educational system did not deter Mark Clark from getting an education. He continuously educated himself utilizing his mother's large collection of encyclopedias. He studied the encyclopedias constantly and often shared what he learned. Anthropology and History were among the topics he enjoyed most. Mark talked about the injustice done to Indigenous people, Africans, and Aboriginals. He especially admired the Native American Leader Geronimo because Geronimo refused to accept existence on the reservation.

Mark's older siblings became much more influential during his teenage years. When older brother George came home on leave from his duties as a Military Policeman, he felt the need to train his younger brother in survival skills. On one occasion, George's training involved Mark sitting in a chair while George choked him. The goal was to see how long Mark could last without flinching. As George continued choking him, he did not flinch. Mark never flinched and eventually fell to the floor not moving and barely breathing. With siblings screaming and thinking Mark was dead, he eventually recovered after several minutes. This would not be the last of Mark's training. His older brothers would continue preparing him for the struggle.

Older brothers James and Matthew were especially influential. They were both highly intelligent and enjoyed imparting knowledge. Matt and James were popular young men. Nearly all the black families in Peoria knew who they were, or knew they were among the numerous Clark siblings. James was strong-willed with a seemly hard exterior. He could easily intimidate a person. Matthew spoke in smooth flowing language and wore the most stylish clothing. He was a good fighter who developed a reputation for giving out plenty of hooks and jabs. Matthew's friend, comedian Richard Pryor once described him in a comedic routine saying "Matt was bad; knocking mother fuckers out...He was a killer, Jack".

Mathew and James were both tough industrious young men, determined to survive the system. They ventured into the Peoria streets where they were exposed to many vices. Elder Clark and Mother Clark cautioned their children many times about the dangers of the Peoria streets. Mother Clark called it "A Den of Iniquity". Peoria was famous for its numerous alcohol distilleries; and red light districts where drugs, prostitution, and crime seemed to go hand and hand. James and Matthew would be drawn into the Peoria street life and begin hustling at pool halls and after-hour juke joints.

They would provide their brother Mark with an education in street life.

In January 1962, the only grandfather the Clark children had ever known passed away. Elder Clark's father, Alex Clark Sr. died. He was born in 1885, the son of Caroline Conner and Louis Clark. Alex Clark Sr. married Rena (Hullum) Clark in the early 1900's. He fathered thirteen children. Alex Clark Sr. was 76 years old at the time of his death. The Clark family traveled to Memphis, Tennessee for his Home Going Service. Elder William Clark Sr. grieved the loss of his beloved father. The entire Clark family mourned his passing and reverenced his memory as the first patriarch of the Clark family.

By 1962, the Civil Rights Movement expanded its integration campaign and began focusing more attention toward economic empowerment. The collective response of the Black Church and organizations like SNCC, SCLC, CORE and NAACP helped achieve successes and legislative changes. The rise of religious leaders, nationalist groups, and other grassroots activists helped focus attention toward the economic needs of black people.

Elder William Clark Sr.
and other Ministers.

In Chicago, COGIC Bishop of Illinois, Louis Henry Ford and Bishop Eleazar Lenox were determined to increase COGIC participation in civil rights initiatives. The Bishops promoted the formation of an Interdenominational Ministers Alliance. Elder William Clark Sr. was commissioned to organize the Ministers Alliance in the Greater Central Illinois District. Elder Clark served as

President of the Interdenominational Ministers Alliance; meeting with clergy from Pentecostal, Apostolic, Baptist, and Non-denominational churches throughout Central Illinois. The religious leaders called upon local businesses to extend more job opportunities and end redlining of housing for the disenfranchised in the inner-cities.

In Cairo, Illinois Reverend Blaine Ramsey Jr., was a Minister at Ward Chapel African Methodist Episcopal Church. He was Vice-president of the Cairo NAACP; and he was a member of the Interdenominational Ministers Alliance in Cairo. Reverend Ramsey and members of the Ministers Alliance demanded the city begin permanent employment of black workers and end discriminatory hiring practices. He reached out to activists with SNCC's direct action wing. Activists came to Cairo, Illinois and mounted a protest against segregation. This was the first integration campaign north of the Ohio River.

Charles Koen was a youth Minister at the time in Cairo and he represented the youth protestors boycotting businesses throughout the city. He would later found the organization The United Front. After a black youth protestor was murdered under suspicious circumstances, Cairo, Illinois ignited in youth rebellion. Eventually, the National Guard was called out. The activism and demands of the youth in Cairo helped spark the Civil Rights Movement in Southern Illinois.

In Peoria during the early 1960's Matthew Clark was Youth Coordinator for the local Chapter of the NAACP. Samuel, James and Charles Clark were members. John Gwynn was President of the Peoria, Illinois Chapter of the NAACP; and Sam Polk was Vice-President. In 1962, Matthew Clark, John Gwynn, and several other members of the Peoria NAACP were in the middle of their meeting at a local church when they received a frantic knock at the door. It was a Chaplain from a nearby prison who had been informed black people were in danger; and he wanted the NAACP's help.

After the Chaplain briefly explained the dire circumstances, Matthew, John Gwynn, and two others followed him to a location about 30 miles outside of Peoria. In the woods they came upon an old dilapidated structure guarded by a number of white men holding shotguns. As the NAACP group and Chaplain approached, he announced to the white men that they should let the people go who were forced to work there. The white men shouted back that everyone working there wanted to be there. With weapons drawn, the white men demanded that the Chaplain and NAACP group get off the property. After a brief standoff, the local Sherriff pulled up. When the Sherriff came and learned that the group asking questions was the NAACP, he attempted to downplay the situation. He allowed the NAACP men to go inside and check on the people. As soon as the Sherriff opened the door, the smell left no doubt in Matthew's mind it was modern-day slavery. The people were barely alive and living in horrific conditions. The Sherriff denied that they were being kept against their will and he said they could have left if they wanted to. The workers didn't leave but it was obvious that they couldn't.

The next day Matthew Clark and the other NAACP Leaders called up everybody they knew; and not all their calls went out to NAACP members. Within several hours they gathered together about sixty cars of black men armed to the teeth. They led the sixty-car caravan back out into the woods to go rescue the workers. As soon as the white men saw all the cars full of black men approaching, they took off running and hiding with their Smith and Wesson long barrel shotguns. They locked themselves in a large shed. NAACP President John Gwynn prevented the black men from burning down the shed where the white men were hiding.

The workers who were being held were brought back to Peoria. They were taken to a local church where they were provided food and medical aide. By Sunday, they were taken in by various people in the church congregations. It was discovered the workers were from North Carolina and were brought by bus to Illinois and forced to work hard labor. After this incident, the Peoria Chapter of the NAACP became even more prominent in the community.

The Peoria Chapter of the NAACP began actively participating in civil rights initiatives including sit-ins, boycotts, and demonstrations. NAACP President John Gwynn took notice of how many of the older Clark siblings participated in the Civil Rights Movement. Gwynn described the Clark's as "alert and knowledgeable on the issues". In 1963, Mark Clark joined his older brothers in the local Peoria Chapter of the NAACP. He was fifteen years old when he joined.

Mark began protesting and boycotting businesses throughout Peoria. He participated in the *Peoria Bus Boycott* in June 1963; two months before the *March on Washington for Jobs and Freedom.* The Peoria Bus Boycott began in response to the assassination of Medgar Evers, President of the NAACP Jackson, Mississippi Chapter. Mark Clark demanded economic justice, jobs, housing, and freedom. He exhibited great leadership qualities and a substantial ability to influence youth. NAACP Chapter President, John Gwynn described Mark Clark as a person of action, and he once said, "He could call for order when older persons or adults could not."

During the Peoria Bus Boycott, Elder Clark's Lincoln Avenue Church of God in Christ was a rallying point. Mathew Clark recalled how he and his brothers, and other boycotters met up at their father's church to prepare for protests. Like most COGIC preachers, Elder Clark believed in civil rights but was not actually comfortable with protests and boycotts. Mathew recalls an influential conversation that he had with his father. The conversation was about how Elder Clark had a duty to support the boycotts and protests because he was the President of the Ministers Alliance in Peoria. Their conversation prompted

Elder Clark to allow his sons the use of his church for the rally. Mathew would never forget how his father received flak from law enforcement officials about the numerous boycotters.

Several months after the Peoria Bus Boycott, Dr. Martin Luther King, Jr. led the *March on Washington for Jobs and Freedom*. The march took place August 1963 in Washington D.C. at the front of the Lincoln Memorial. Dr. King's historic and heartfelt "I have a Dream" was heard before an audience of more than 250,000 people. It was the largest civil rights gathering in history at that time. The success of the *March on Washington for Jobs and Freedom* led to the passage of the Civil Rights Act of 1964.

In Peoria, Mark and his brothers; Samuel, Mathew, James, and Charles would go on to protest and boycott other businesses. With their participation the Peoria Chapter of the NAACP would take part in protests at CILCO, the Pere Marquette Hotel, and Peoria Water Works. Peoria inner-city youth would actively participate in the nation's Freedom Summer as blacks engaged in mass sit-ins and demonstrations.

In 1964, the Big-B Barber Shop at Bradley University was among the targets of NAACP youth protests. The Big-B refused service to blacks and required Bradley University black student basketball players to come in through the back door. Mark and the other inner-city youth would congregate in the streets near Bradley University to protest. The NAACP was involved in legal actions against Bradley University and Big-B Barber Shop. Eventually, the Big-B suffered fire damage when a protestor threw a Molotov cocktail into the establishment.

The FBI Counter Intelligence Program launched a campaign against civil rights activists and nationalist organizations. Since its inception, the FBI targeted prominent black leaders considered influential. They deemed influential black leaders part of a subversive threat to the security of the United States of America. Common accusations were suspected un-American or Communist activities. In the early years of the twentieth century, black leaders targeted by the FBI were W.E.B. DuBois, The Honorable Marcus Mosiah Garvey, Paul Robeson, The Most Honorable Elijah Muhammad, Bishop Charles H. Mason Sr., and many more. As organizations, activists, and black religious leaders began to speak out more forcefully, J. Edgar Hoover deemed them as Black Nationalists and described their organizations as Hate Groups. Among those targeted by Hoover during the Civil Rights Movement were SNCC Leader, Stokely Carmichael (Kwame Ture); SCLC Leader, Reverend Dr. Martin Luther King Jr., and Organization for Afro-American Unity Leader, Malcolm X (El Hajj Malik El Shabazz).

Chapter 5.

Movements, Empowerment and Police

Movements, Empowerment, and Police

In 1965, Malcolm X, the former Nation of Islam Leader was assassinated at the Audubon Ball Room in Washington Heights, New York. His home had been firebomb one week prior to his assassination. The year prior to his death, he formed the Organization for Afro-American Unity and established ties with the members of SNCC. His funeral service was held in Harlem at Childs Memorial Temple Church of God in Christ.

The Chicago Freedom Movement began in 1965. The movement started as a large rally in Chicago, Illinois when African American's began demanding open housing, education, transportation, health, wealth generation, and criminal justice reform. During that time, COGIC Bishop Louis Henry Ford took a prominent role as co-Chairman of the 1965 Chicago Conference. He actively worked with civic and political organizations and once said "We stay in the grassroots and do not run from ourselves" when explaining the growth of his church.

Bishop Ford's active participation in civil rights gave encouragement to COGIC members to participate. With the events of Bloody Sunday and the brutal treatment of nonviolent civil rights activists marching on the Edmund Pettis Bridge still fresh in their minds, members of COGIC began actively supporting the nonviolent wing of the Civil Rights Movement. Increasingly, they joined the ranks of the NAACP.

In January of 1966, Reverend Dr. Martin Luther King, Jr. came to Chicago. He moved into a tenant flat on Chicago's west side to demonstrate poor living conditions and organize efforts to end slum housing. While living in Chicago, Dr. King began an Interfaith Economic Justice Program called Operation Breadbasket. It started in Atlanta and he sent Reverend Jesse Jackson to launch it in Chicago. Operation Breadbasket negotiated with companies for jobs, services, and products.

Dr. Martin Luther King Jr. and his wife Coretta Scott King visited the campus of Illinois Wesleyan College, a private Christian college in Bloomington, Illinois. The College was made up almost exclusively of white students. At the time of his visit to Wesleyan, Mark's sister Patricia Clark was active in the NAACP and a college student at nearby Illinois State University. When she learned that Dr. King would be speaking, she attended the event held at Fred Young Field House on February 10, 1966. Pat recalled that Dr. King's speech stressed Justice. His delivery and vocabulary were highly impressive, even to college students. Seeing and hearing Dr. King in person was an electrifying experience.

Dr. King's speech was about whether or not there had been any progress in race relations. Reverend King discussed the positions taken by both the optimist and the pessimist. He agreed with the optimist that blacks have come a long way, and with the pessimist that blacks have a long way to go. Dr. King's speech focused on time, legislation, and the need for nonviolent direct action. Of Time he said, "Somewhere we must come to see that human progress never roles in on the wheels of inevitability, it comes through the tireless efforts and the persistent work of dedicated individuals who are willing to be co-workers with God". Of legislation he said, "There may be some truth that you can't legislate integration, but you can legislate segregation". Dr. King went on to say, "Legislation can't change the heart, but it can restrain the heartless". "It might not change the hearts of men, but it will change the habits of men". Dr. King closed his speech urging the community to engage in nonviolent direct action. He called it the most potent weapon to disarm the opponent and work on their moral conscience. Dr. King said, it was either "nonviolence or nonexistence".

That same week, Patricia returned home to Peoria. She joined the rest of the Clark family in celebration of Elder Clark's founding of a new church building and his twenty years of Pastoral Leadership. Members of Lincoln Avenue COGIC were clothed in white garments to represent the Holiness of the Saints. They marched in unison from the Lincoln Avenue church to the new church building, ten blocks away. The Dedication Services were officiated by Bishop Eleazer Lenox of the Southern Illinois Ecclesiastical Jurisdiction of the COGIC. The new church building was located at 228 South Webster Street; and was incorporated as Holy Temple Church of God in Christ in Peoria, Illinois.

Holy Temple 1966 Dedication Book

    The new church building was a blessing to the community. It was a large stone edifice with seating for up to five hundred people. The church was equipped with an enclosed nursery for children, baptismal pool, balcony, kitchen, dining hall, and plenty of meeting rooms.

Mother Fannie Mae Clark and Elder William Clark Sr. at Holy Temple COGIC Dedication Services February 1966.

Next door to the church was a parsonage home for Elder Clark and his family to reside. The McBean Street parsonage was a two-story house with bedrooms and bathrooms upstairs and down. While residing at the parsonage

Elder Clark was able to keep the doors of the church open almost continuously while watching over his large household. The doors of the church opened promptly for prayer, consecration, and for ministry and missions.

Elders and Ministers of the Church of God in Christ Elder Williams, Elder Felton Beck Sr., Minister Artis, Elder J.R Hicks., Assistant Pastor, Minister Omie Taylor, and Minister Chester Warr.

Deacons of Holy Temple COGIC

Mothers Board of Holy Temple COGIC
Front row: Mother Flowers and Mother Hollis
Back row: Mother Johnson, Mother Danage,
Mother Artis, and Mother Hunter

Usher Board at Holy Temple COGIC

Elder Monroe Williams
Playing electric guitar at Holy Temple COGIC

Clark Quartet (Luke Clark, Robert Clark, Rose Clark and John Clark)

Patricia Clark serving dinner after church services. Mother Fannie Mae Clark, Elder Evans and others are shown sitting.

Mark Clark was eighteen years old when he celebrated the founding of Holy Temple COGIC with his family. He was proud of his father's twenty years of Pastoral Leadership and his role as a servant leader. As Superintendent of the Greater Central Illinois District and President of the Ministers Alliance, Elder William Clark Sr. was actively engaged in improving the social and economic conditions of the people.

Over the next several months, Mark Clark and the rest of the Clark family would watch the news as Dr. Martin Luther King Jr. led protests for jobs, housing, and economic empowerment in the State of Illinois. In August of 1966, Reverend Dr. Martin Luther King, Jr. was struck in the head with a stone in Chicago's Marquette Park. Dr. King stated "I have seen many demonstrations in the south, but I have never seen anything hostile and so hateful as I've seen here today". The treatment of Dr. King disturbed many in the community, including Mother Fannie Mae Clark. She said the treatment of Dr. King was "A shame and a disgrace". It was a glaring reminder of how even nonviolent African American religious leaders were beaten and brutalized for demanding equal rights. Mark Clark observed how the brutality against Dr. King affected his mother and the whole community. The backlash from angry whites and police seemed to fuel the rise of more civil rights activists and other Black Nationalist organizations.

In October of 1966, in Oakland, California; the Black Panther Party for Self-Defense was formed by Huey Newton and Bobby Seale. The two African American college students examined the capitalist structure, the relation of class and race, economics, and culture. The organization adopted the Black Panther symbol from an independent political party formed by residents in Lowndes County, Alabama. To emphasize their commitment, the aesthetics Black Panthers wore consisted of the black leather jacket, black beret, combat boots, and fatigues. As a Black Panther Party recruit, one would make a commitment to struggle for the people; and to fight for liberation and human rights.

The Black Panther Party for Self-Defense developed a program of community-based policing. Black Panthers engaged in direct confrontation with police to prevent brutality. They implemented community initiatives such as protesting rent evictions, demanding school traffic lights, informing welfare recipients of their legal rights, and teaching classes in history. The Black Panther Party for Self Defense introduced The Ten Point Program and platform demanding freedom, full employment, end of capitalist robbery, housing, education, military exemption, end to police brutality, prison reform, trial by peers, and land. The black revolutionaries emphasized self-reliance, self-defense against police brutality, and the need for a common struggle for justice. They created community-based programs such as the Free Breakfast Program, Free Medical Clinic, and Sickle Cell Anemia Testing. By 1967, the Black Panther Party dropped "For Self Defense" from its title.

In 1967, a former affiliate of Malcolm X Organization of Afro-American Unity and author of the book *Soul on Ice* joined the Black Panther Party becoming its Minister of Information. Eldridge Cleaver and his wife Kathleen Cleaver became prominent figures in the organization helping to increase its visibility and popularity. Cleaver used provocative and explicit language describing the police as fascist pigs. The use of explicit language and imagery sold newspapers and helped recruit the proletariat. The Panther Newspaper images of Black Panther Party members holding weapons for self-defense reinforced that they were protectors of the community. The portrayal of Black Panther Party Leader and Minister of Defense, Huey Newton sitting in a wicker chair became the iconic image symbolic of his role as Leader of the Black Power Liberation Struggle.

The heightening media interest led to increased demands for Black Panther Party Leaders to participate in interviews and speaking engagements at Colleges and Universities. During those events, Black Panther Party Leaders used rhetoric and oratory as they expounded on their political beliefs. They spoke out against the injustices of the capitalist structure and for self-reliance, black empowerment, and the need for a proletarian revolution.

Meanwhile, in Peoria, Illinois the atmosphere was ripe with tension. Law abiding African Americans were monitored and harassed by Peoria Police, which often led to arbitrary restrictions on activities and bogus criminal charges. Due to unfair arrests, Elder

William Clark was called upon to help get members of his church out of jail. He was a trusted confidant and a paramount spokesman for his church congregation. Elder Clark would certainly speak prudently on their behalf.

Elder William Clark Sr.

Telephone calls and visits from Peoria Police were frequent occurrences at Holy Temple COGIC. Periodically, the police would knock on the door of the church in the middle of the Sunday night sermon; requesting the members to quiet down. Elder Clark would question the unfairness of why his church was being monitored but taverns full of noisy partiers were allowed to stay open all night long. He was a man of God who was steadfast in his ministry and he was not going to quench the Holy Ghost. As soon as the police would leave, Elder Clark would walk to the back of the church and fling the doors of Holy Temple open wide. He continued to preach so that his sermon could be heard throughout the neighborhood.

Holy Temple members usually responded to the police activity by watching attentively and looking at one another in astonishment. They would give Elder Clark words of encouragement such as "Go Head, Now! ", and "Preach, Preacher!". The congregation would continue to praise God with electric guitars, drums, piano, singing, hand-clapping, tambourines, and praise dancing in the Sanctified tradition. Some in the congregation would jump up and down and others were led by the spirit to walk back and forth down the church isles.

The Clark's traveled with the Holy Temple congregation to churches throughout the State of Illinois. In 1967 they traveled to Springfield, Illinois to the spring State Meeting.

When the Clark family stayed in Springfield they resided as guests in the Minister's home near the church. In 1967, Mark's younger brother Johnny Clark attended. He played piano and sung with his siblings in the Clark Quartet. He was twelve years old at the time. He looked forward to performing with the group during the State Meeting in Springfield. He also wanted to attend to visit with his friends who were sons of other Ministers.

During the State Holy Convocation, church services lasted nearly all day long. Eventually, Johnny and several other boys left church and went outside to socialize. In a yard nearby, they met another boy with several bicycles who allowed them to ride. For a short while, the boys rode around the neighborhood. They were soon stopped by the Springfield Police who falsely accused them of stealing bicycles. The boys were taken to the Springfield Police Station where they were interrogated and held. When Elder Clark and the other Ministers learned that their sons were taken to jail, they quickly went to the Springfield Police Station to get the boys out.

Johnny was placed in a separate room from the other boys. He recalled that when the police interrogated him he could not answer anything. He was frightened and didn't know the address where he was staying in Springfield. He could hear what was going on in the other room and what he heard disturbed him. The police officer told the Ministers to beat their sons. He listened as a police officer took off his belt to give to the Ministers. As Johnny listened in, he heard two of the Ministers actually beating their son's right in the next room. After hearing the other boys yelling out and getting whipped by their fathers, he worried about what was going to happen to him. He knew his father was a disciplinarian with a thick leather belt.

When Elder Clark came into the room he saw the frightened look on his son's face. He told his son, "let's go" and they walked out of the Springfield Police Station together. Johnny dreaded that at any moment he would get it from his father. He stayed in the guest bedroom and he didn't come out. Mother Clark came in the room and asked if he was hungry. Johnny was hungry but he was afraid to show himself for fear of Elder Clark. All night long, he stayed in the room. Eventually, he came out when it was time for the family to leave Springfield. Elder Clark never spoke of the matter again. He knew that Johnny had good character and was a victim of circumstance. Elder William Clark Sr. was a disciplinarian but he was a wise and caring father.

The actions of the Springfield Police were indicative of how black people were treated by most law enforcement in the 1960's. Springfield, Illinois was no different from other cities except that it was the site of the NAACP's first Negro Conference on Racial Justice in 1909. The NAACP organization was developed in Springfield after a race riot in 1908 that left eight black people dead.

In 1967, there were protests all over the nation. In Detroit, Michigan it was termed the Long Hot Summer of 1967. African American youth protested and vented their frustrations. Police branded youth as criminals and thugs. Youth who participated in protests and demonstrations were considered to be rioters for demanding jobs, housing, and freedom. In many cases, more vocal African American youth were charged and convicted of criminal offenses resulting in juvenile detention and prison incarceration. By the end of the year, Mark Clark would be charged with disorderly conduct and curfew violations. His older brothers James and Mathew would both be charged with felonies. By the end of the year, Mathew and James would be incarcerated at the Illinois State Correctional Facility.

Chapter 6.

The Year That Was 1968

The Year That Was 1968

Mark Clark began attending Illinois Central College in East Peoria, Illinois. He led youth protests for civil rights on campus. Other civil rights protests were occurring at college campuses and universities all over the nation. There were many activist groups and Black Nationalist organizations protesting injustice and the war in Vietnam. The Black Power Liberation Movement was gaining notoriety and the Black Panther Party was emerging as the central revolutionary organization in the Black Power Liberation Struggle.

The protests at colleges and universities were monitored closely by the Clark's. There were civil rights protests in South Carolina. Police actions left three college students dead. Other disturbances occurred at the University of Wisconsin-Madison and the University of North Carolina at Chapel Hill. Students at Howard University in Washington, DC staged rallies, protests, and a five day sit-in; shutting the university down. The students were protesting the lack of Afrocentric studies and the Vietnam War. Students at Columbia University in New

York took over the administration building in protest of the Vietnam War.

In 1968, Mark Clark's sister, Patricia was in her third year at Illinois State University. On weekends, the family would drive up to Normal, Illinois to visit her in the dormitory to make sure she was alright. Mark and several of his older brothers made trips to the campus to check on her too. When Mark came to Illinois State University, he usually protested for civil rights, socialized on campus, and dated his sister's college friends.

Around that time members from the Black Panther Party and other Black Power Liberation Movements held a Free Huey rally at the Alameda County Courthouse in Oakland, California. The rally was in support of Huey Newton, Black Panther Party Leader and Minister of Defense who was charged with murdering a police officer. Black Panther Party Chairman Bobby Seale spoke, along with H. Rap Brown (Jamil Al-Amin), and Stokely Carmichael. James Forman, Alprentice "Bunchy" Carter, and Eldridge Cleaver were among the attendees at the rally. The event was one of the largest to ever take place in Oakland.

Bobby Seale and Huey Newton

The rally's success was proof that Huey Newton, Black Panther Party Minister of Defense was the central leader of the revolutionary movement. This event signaled the SNCC-Panther alliance that was forming to unify the Black Power Liberation Struggle.

During that time, a government report was released entitled The Kerner Commission Report. The report talked about the causes of the 1967 protests and riots. According to their findings, it resulted from black frustrations at the lack of economic opportunities. The report blamed the federal and state government for failed housing programs, education, and social service policies. The document was critical of the main stream media for their perspective and said the cause of much of the urban violence was white racism. It said the remedy for the problem was creating jobs, housing, and ending segregation. The report concluded "America was moving toward two societies; one black, one white, separate, and unequal"

In Memphis, Tennessee two African American sanitation workers were crushed to death in garbage trucks. After their deaths, over 1,000 black sanitation workers began striking. Members of the Church of God in Christ in Memphis played a central role in supporting the strike. Mason Temple became the site of marches, rallies, and police intimidation. The *Memphis Sanitation Workers Strike* was one of the most significant events indicative of the involvement of the COGIC during the Civil Rights Movement.

On February 24, 1968, Reverend James Lawson led Ministers and marchers from City Auditorium to Mason Temple as part of the *Memphis Sanitation Workers Strike*. Police began disrupting the march and used their police cars to push marchers; eventually injuring a marcher by running over their foot with the police car. As protestors marched outside Mason Temple, police began spraying mace in the eyes of the Ministers and the elderly men and women who marched. After the abuse that the marchers endured, COGIC Elder G.E. Patterson and other Ministers called for an immediate meeting. That evening, the Ministers formed the organization Community On the Move for Equality (COME). The following day, Bishop J.O. Patterson Sr. joined Reverend Lawson for a press conference announcing the formation of the organization. The COME leaders spearheaded rallies and economic boycotts of businesses and its formation put COGIC at the forefront of the *Memphis Sanitation Workers Strike*. In an effort to help fight for better working conditions, Dr. Martin Luther King Jr. would join their strike one month later. That same month, FBI Director J. Edgar Hoover defined the goals of COINTELPRO.

In March 1968, FBI Director, Hoover wrote the following memo..."COINTELPRO defines its goals as preventing coalitions between black militant groups, the rise of a messiah who could unify and electrify the black masses, and as discrediting and preventing the growth of Black Nationalist organizations". Hoover's memo led to the targeting of African American church leaders and activists all across the nation. They would become targets of the FBI, Justice Department, and law enforcement officials in an effort to prevent the rise of a Black Messiah. The directive resulted in a systematic process of threats, surveillance, misinformation campaigns, and assassinations of law abiding African American activists and religious leaders.

Reverend Dr. Martin Luther King, Jr. became a target of the FBI's COINTELPRO because of his ability to influence and unify the masses thru nonviolent protests. The success of the Montgomery Bus Boycott in the 1950's placed him squarely on Hoover's FBI target list. Dr. King*'s March on Washington for Jobs and Freedom* led to the passage of the Civil Rights Act of 1964, the Voting Rights Act of 1965, and a Nobel Peace Prize for combating racial inequality. These achievements infuriated J. Edgar Hoover who deemed Dr. King as "The Most Dangerous Negro in the Future of the Nation". Hoover's personal vendetta against Dr. Martin Luther King, Jr. resulted in the FBI's use of nefarious tactics designed to discredit and destroy him. There tactics did not deter Dr. King from continuing his coalition building activities. He led nonviolent protests across the nation, demanded better jobs, improved pay, better working conditions, and bringing an end to slum housing. Reverend Dr. Martin Luther King Jr. joined many initiatives; including *The Chicago Freedom Movement* and the *Memphis Sanitation Workers Strike.*

One month after Hoover wrote the infamous FBI memo, Reverend Dr. Martin Luther King Jr. delivered his "Mountain Top" sermon at Mason Temple COGIC in Memphis. Dr. King told the Ministers at Mason Temple that they should not let the court injunctions turn them around. Dr. King said that the Preachers must tell about injustice and that like Jesus, they were anointed to deal with the problems of the poor. He reminded the Ministers at Mason Temple that it was alright to preach about heaven but their mission was to be concerned about the slums on Earth. In his speech, he encouraged the community to use their economic buying power and withdraw support from businesses and financial institutions that did not support black people. Reverend Dr. Martin Luther King Jr. was assassinated the next day, April 4, 1968 at the Loraine Motel in Memphis.

After Dr. King's assassination, protests broke out in cities and towns all over the United States of America. On the campus of Illinois State University, Patricia Clark and other college students protested his assassination. In Peoria, all the older Clark brothers protested and demonstrated in the streets. Mark was so infuriated until his revolutionary spirit boiled up and came forth. He led youth protests throughout the city. In Taft Homes, a public housing project, youth threw bricks and bottles resulting in injury to over ten people; including police officers.

Two days after the assassination of Dr. Martin Luther King Jr., Oakland police murdered seventeen year old Bobby Hutton, the Treasurer and first recruit into the Black Panther Party. Months later, government chaos ensued when the U.S. Democratic Presidential candidate was assassinated. Robert Kennedy's assassination led many to question if it was planned by operatives of the government to affect the outcome of the U.S. Presidential election. Chaos continued further, when police clashed with anti-war protestors at the Democratic National Convention in Chicago, Illinois. The protest erupted after an announcement that the Department of Defense would be sending troops back to Vietnam for a second involuntary tour of duty. Black Panther Party Chairman, Bobby Seale was arrested during the protest.

With the death of Martin Luther King Jr., came the fear of violence against other black religious leaders, activists and Black Nationalists. This fractured much of the coordination between religious and nationalists groups. The use of profanity, calling police names such as fascist pigs, and raising fists as a symbol of Black Power were characterized by many religious people as against the teachings of racial reconciliation and nonviolence. Some Preachers who were known to embrace economic empowerment and self-reliance were not in agreement with the provocative language of the black revolutionaries. The Black Church began distancing itself from the Black Power Liberation Movement. Most churches abandoned their community-based economic empowerment programs.

When most Black Churches began distancing themselves from the Civil Rights Movement, a few stayed in the grassroots. Reverend Blaine Ramsey Jr., Pastor of Ward Chapel AME Church began working with black revolutionaries and supporting their demands. Reverend Ramsey was the former Minister of Ward Chapel AME in Cairo, Illinois. He was instrumental in obtaining an agreement with the Illinois Council of Churches to provide a network for feeding the poor and assisting the impoverished communities.

Meanwhile, the Clark's were welcoming home their oldest son William Clark Jr. He returned home from the war in Vietnam after receiving a medical discharge. He was critically burned over a large part of his body after a water tank blew up in his barracks. He told the family of his ordeal and how he was flown to Japan and hospitalized for several months. Each day in the burn unit, he and the other patients talked each other through the pain they were about to endure. Nurses would scrape their wounds daily and apply a medication referred to as White Lighting. The daily scraping and applying of medicine brought on almost unbearable pain but the process was known to be one of the most effective treatments for healing burn wounds. While in his hospital bed, William Jr. vowed that if he ever made it back home again from the war he would follow the spiritual path set by his father.

Mark and the other siblings listened attentively as their older brother described the horrors of war. William Jr. talked about the millions of tons of bombs dropped by the U.S. and the horrific after-effects of the Agent Orange used to clear the jungle and deny cover to the Viet Cong. He talked about the tenacity of the North Vietnamese people for their guerilla war tactics, fighting off the superpowers, and their construction of the Ho Chi Minh trail.

William Jr. moved into the family's old Seventh Street home not long after returning from the war. Before long, Mark and several of the other Clark's moved in. When the Clark brothers weren't discussing serious matters like war, politics and religion, they were spending time socializing and playing pinochle, a card game William Jr. learned in the army. All of the Clark brothers were athletic and they enjoyed playing basketball, football, baseball, and tennis. When the brothers weren't playing sports with one another, they were watching sports.

Whenever the *Wide World of Sports* was broadcast, the Clark brothers were fixed to the little black and white TV screen. The Clark's enjoyed watching boxing matches and track and field competitions where black athletes usually performed. All of the Clark family admired boxing champion Muhammad Ali, not just because of his boxing skills. The Clark's admired his ability to talk boldly and unapologetically. They respected his decision to join the Nation of Islam and become a conscientious objector refusing to be drafted into the U.S. Armed Forces. In fact, the Clark family had so much respect for Muhammad Ali that it didn't bother them that much when Ali defeated a Clark relative, Heavy-Weight Boxer Ernie Terrell in 1967.

The Clark family watched *Wide World of Sports* TV coverage during the 19th Olympiad held in Mexico City. They applauded the two African American Olympians, Tommie Smith and John Carlos as they raised their fists in the Black Power Salute after winning gold and bronze medals. The two sports figures used their platform as Olympians to bring attention to the struggles of black people. The photographs of their controversial actions were displayed all around the world becoming the most iconic photograph ever taken at a sporting event. It was inspiring to black youth all across the nation.

Sadly, on November 3, 1968, the Clark family experienced the loss of Fannie Mae Clark's mother, Ella (Terrell) Bardley. She was born in 1894, the daughter of Lovett Terrell Sr. and Fannie Brewer. Ella Bardley was the driving force in her family's migration from the south during the Great Migration. She helped raise her seventeen Clark grandchildren and was their last living grandparent. Ella (Terrell) Bardley's Home Going Service was held at Grace Baptist Church in Peoria, Illinois. She was a founding member of the church and attended faithfully for many years. Mother Fannie Mae Clark wept silently for her beloved mother. Elder Clark wept aloud to express the enormous grief at the loss of his mother-in-law. Mark Clark and all the rest of the Clark family, relatives, friends, and neighbors mourned her loss and grieved many years. Her final resting place is Springdale Cemetery in Peoria, Illinois.

By late 1968, a student at Triton Junior College, Chairman Fred Hampton Sr., co-founded the Chicago, Illinois Chapter of the Black Panther Party. The Chicago, Illinois Black Panther Party Leader was a former NAACP Youth Council Leader. Chairman Fred was highly intelligent and among his areas of study were law and politics. Chairman Fred Hampton Sr. had charisma and was an excellent speaker. He was responsible for establishing the original Rainbow Coalition motivating and unifying inner-city youth, street gangs, activists, and nationalists. The Black Panther Party Leader taught political education classes, heightening interest and support for the Black Power Liberation Struggle.

During speaking engagements, Chairman Fred would expound on his revolutionary ideals; delivering thought-provoking statements and his own famous firebrand quotations. Among them was his phrase "You can kill a revolutionary; but you can't kill the revolution". Black nationalists, socialists, and revolutionary organizations were attracted to his message. Chairman Fred would work to establish the Black Panther Party Free People's Clinic and Free People's Breakfast Program in Chicago. Leadership of the Black Panther Party planned to appoint Chairman Fred Hampton Sr. as Chief of Staff of the Party's Central Committee. The FBI COINTELPRO planned to assassinate him; identifying him as a potential Black Messiah because of his influence in the community.

FRED HAMPTON

Fred Hampton was a high school student and a promising leader when he joined the Black Panther Party at the age of 19. His status as a leader grew very quickly. By the age of 20 he became the leader for the Chicago Chapter of the Black Panther Party. He was involved in a lot of activities to improve the black community in Chicago. He maintained regular speaking engagements and organized weekly rallies at the Chicago federal building on behalf of the BPP. He worked with a Free People's Clinic, taught political education classes every morning at 6am, and launched a community control of police project. Hampton was also instrumental in the BPP's Free Breakfast Program. Hampton had the charisma to excite crowds during rallies; he was suppose to be appointed to the Party's Central Committee. His position would have been Chief of Staff if he did not have an untimely death on the evening of December 4, 1969.

Events Leading up to The Death of Fred Hampton

The social climate of the late 1960s was definitely NOT on Hampton's side. The government was not supportive of any radical political organization, and in fact turned out to be downright suspicious at any attempt to challenge or change the status-quo. Discriminating against the black community was the norm. When word of a "Days of Rage" rally came to the government's attention, it was known that some members of the BPP supported this "attack on the pig power structure." Allegedly, Fred Hampton and the majority of the Chicago Panthers did not support this rally, but to the FBI they were guilty by association. This information, combined with the general suspicion the government had of the BPP, and Fred's powerful speaking and organizing skills, made Fred Hampton a wanted man. The Federal Bureau of Investigation saw Fred Hampton as a threat to society that needed to be eliminated. They conspired with the Chicago Police Department (CPD) and William O'Neal to spy on Fred to give them information about his daily itinerary in order to have O'Neal's felony charges dropped. His job was to serve as a bodyguard of Fred and director of the Chapter's security. He was suppose to notify the FBI of the Panther's apartment floor plan and how many residents lived in the apartment. When the FBI got its information a raid was authorized by the state attorney Hanrahan. FBI special agents sent a memo to J. Edgar Hoover stating that "a positive course of action [was] being effected under the counterintelligence program." (quoted information from Shane Smith's Fred Hampton Page)

That Unforgettable Morning

That evening Fred Hampton and several Party members including William O'Neal came home to the BPP Headquarters after a political education class. O'Neal volunteered to make the group dinner. He slipped a large dose of secobarbital in Fred's kool-aid and left the apartment around 1:30am, a little while later, Fred fell asleep. Around 4:30am on December 4, 1969 the heavily armed Chicago Police attacked the Panthers' apartment. They entered the apartment by kicking the front door down and then shouting Mark Clark pointblank in the chest. Clark was sleeping in the living room with a shotgun in his hand. His reflexes responded by firing one shot at the police before he died. That bullet was then

Chapter 7.

Mark Clark Joins The Black Panther Party

Mark Clark Joins
The Black Panther Party

Defense Captain Mark Clark
Leader of the Peoria, Illinois Chapter
of the Black Panther Party

In late 1968 Henry Howard, a member of the Black Panther Party from Oakland, California came to visit his mother in Peoria, Illinois. She was a member of the COGIC. Her children were Clark family friends since their early years growing up in Elder William Clark's church. Henry knew there were numerous Clark brothers and the oldest William Jr. had plenty of military experience. He visited William Jr. at the Clark's Seventh Street home in an effort to recruit him into the Black Panther Party.

When Henry Howard visited William Jr's., he learned that Mark was living there with his older brother. Henry gave the Clark brothers Black Panther Party literature to read. As William Jr. and Mark reviewed the information, they all engaged in deep conversation. The group talked about the Ten-Point Program and platform, self-reliance, and police brutality. They all expressed outrage over the bogus criminal charges and jail incarcerations of the Black Panther Party members, Minister of Defense Huey Newton, and Chairman Bobby Seale. Henry talked about the need for a common struggle against injustice and a proletarian revolution. Eventually, William Jr. having experienced enough conflict in his twelve years in Korea and Vietnam said that he was planning on becoming a Christian Minister.

Henry Howard took notice of how younger brother, Mark Clark was actively fighting against racism and brutality; and how he was engaging in civil rights protests and other acts of civil disobedience. Mark told Henry how he started in his early teenage years protesting and fighting to improve the plight of the people within the ranks of the NAACP. After the deaths of religious leaders, Malcolm X and Dr. Martin Luther King Jr., Mark developed revolutionary ideals. Now he was full of zeal and determination. He understood the inherent oppression of the capitalist structure and believed revolution was the only way to destroy an oppressive system and establish a system of justice.

After talking with Henry Howard, Mark decided to make a commitment to live, struggle, and die for the people. He packed his bags and traveled with Henry Howard to Oakland, California for an official induction and education with the Central Committee Leadership of the Black Panther Party. When he returned from California, he was thoroughly immersed in the philosophy and rhetoric of the Black Panthers. He was expounding oratory on the Marxist Theory of Capitalism and the conflicts between the social classes; the proletarian and the bourgeoisie.

Defense Captain Mark Clark sold The
Black Panther Party Newspapers in Peoria.

Mark Clark organized the Peoria Chapter of the Black Panther Party in early 1969. He motivated the young inner-city recruits to work hard and dedicate themselves to the Black Panther Party Ten-Point Program, platform, and initiatives. He routinely required the Peoria Black Panther Party recruits to participate in marching exercises designed to help achieve greater discipline and unity. Mark and his recruits monitored the neighborhood to prevent crime and they joined protests for economic empowerment. They encouraged inner-city youth and students at the local High School to get involved in the struggle. They sold the Black Panther Party Newspapers which highlighted the Black Panther Party initiatives and exposed police fascism and brutality. They also sold the Red Book, The Quotations of Chairman Mau Tse-Tung which was popular during the wars in Indochina.

Mark Clark established the Black Panther Party Free Breakfast Program in Peoria. He was concerned about the devastating effects that could occur when youth go to school without a healthy meal essential for growth and development. He met with Reverend Blaine Ramsey Jr. who worked closely with organizations such as NAACP, SNCC and The United Front. After meeting with Black Panther Party Leader, Mark Clark, Reverend Ramsey opened up Ward Chapel African Methodist Church facilities to the Peoria Chapter of the Black Panther Party.

The Peoria Chapter of the Black Panther
Party established a Free Breakfast
Program

Members of the Peoria Chapter of the Black Panther Party prepared Free Breakfast for the children and distributed food bags to needy and elderly in the inner-city community. Eventually, church officials began receiving threats from suspected undercover FBI agents and informants forcing them to discontinue the program.

Defense Captain Mark Clark understood the risks involved with joining the revolutionary organization; yet he never wavered. He was dedicated to the people. When he was called upon by Chairman Fred Hampton Sr. to come to Chicago, he answered the call. Mark traveled back and forth from Peoria to Chicago where he coordinated with Chairman Fred Hampton Sr., and other members of the Black Panther Party. He sometimes brought recruits from the Peoria Chapter to Chicago for political education classes led by Chairman Fred.

Chairman Fred Hampton Sr. had many famous quoted statements. Among them was his statement, "I don't want myself on your mind if you're not going to work for the people. Like we always said, if you're asked to make a commitment at the age of 20, and you say, I don't want to make a commitment only because of the simple reason that I'm too young to die, I want to live a little bit longer. What you did is, you're dead already. You have to understand that people have to pay the price for peace. If you dare to struggle, you dare to win. If you dare not struggle, then dammit - you don't deserve to win. Let me say peace to you if you're willing to fight for it.... Why don't you live for the people, why don't you struggle for the people, why don't you die for the people"!

Defense Captain Mark Clark joined the Black Panther Party at a time when they were the number one target of the FBI's Counter Intelligence Program. By the time he began collaborating with Chairman Fred, the Black Panther Party membership in various Chapters around the country were already infiltrated. In Chicago, since December 1968, informant William O'Neal was snitching. He rose through the ranks of the organization to the position of Head of Security for Chairman Fred Hampton Sr. He informed the FBI about the Panthers that frequented the headquarters of the Chicago Chapter of the Black Panther Party.

By the beginning of 1969, the government's efforts to eliminate the Black Panther Party intensified. Black Panthers Alprentice "Bunchy" Carter and John Higgins were slain at Campbell Hall on the campus of UCLA. Members of the San Diego Black Panther Party were killed selling newspapers. Various other incidents occurred throughout the nation. For this reason, Mark Clark, Leader of the Peoria Chapter of the Black Panther Party made it a point to travel back and forth from Chicago to Peoria in the middle of the night. During that time he was better able to evade authorities.

As the Clark family followed the TV news, they saw how the police were stepping up their campaign against the Black Panther Party. The family was definitely concerned about Mark Clark's safety and security. In March 1969, Mark's mother was beginning breakfast when she heard a noise. Mother Clark walked thru the kitchen, down the basement steps, and yelled out a deep-seated primordial sound. At first, the children thought it was fear that drove her so they called out for Elder Clark; and he came quickly. There at the bottom of the basement steps was Mark Clark hugging his mother. It was apparent then that Mother Clark's yell was an expression of her joy and relief in seeing her son. When Mark's father first saw him he said nothing but relief was written all over his face. Elder Clark and the other family members met Mark at the bottom of the basement steps and they all threw arms around him.

When Mark came home to his family's McBean Street parsonage house next door to Holy Temple COGIC, the entire family was glad to see him. His numerous siblings would pass the word to one another saying "Mark is here". Each of his brothers and sisters would take turns spending personal time with him. Without ever discussing it, the Clark family all knew he wouldn't stay home long. They were satisfied to spend the day together and nobody in the family worried in those moments what might happen next.

Mark Clark's youngest sibling, Rose was ten years old in early 1969. She recalled how Mark talked with her about heavy topics such as African identity. He wanted to make sure she didn't get confused or lose her since of identity with her African ancestral roots. He emphasized to her that whether she was light-skin or dark the system would still work to keep African Americans from unifying the community.

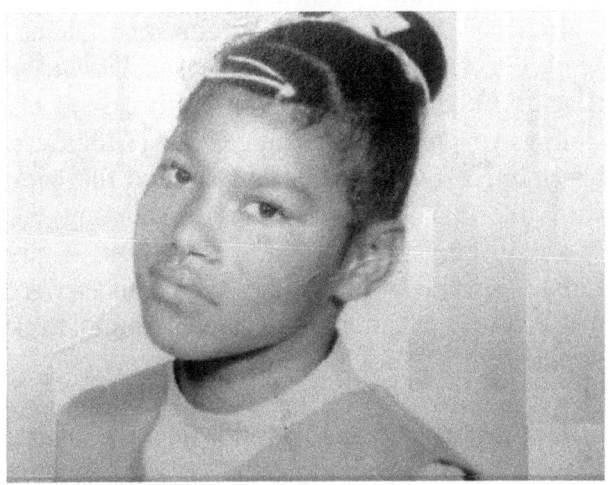

Rose Clark

Mark would asked his little sister serious questions. He often asked, "Whose side will you be on when the revolution comes". Rose recalled being prepared to respond quickly; "I'm going to be on your side when the revolution comes". Upon hearing her reply, Mark would throw up his fist in the Black Power Salute; and he would say "We'll Right On then, Right On!"

Mark Clark brought home the Black Panther Party Newspapers which were required reading materials for his siblings. He made sure the family had a copy of The Red Book of Quotations from Chairman Mao Tse-Tung; which the siblings attempted to comprehend. Mark talked to his brothers and sisters about the Black Panther Party platform and he asked his siblings to join in the struggle. He encouraged his younger siblings to march around the back yard like Black Panther recruits shouting out "To the Left, To the Right, To the Left, Right, Left.". Several of his brothers and a sister were inspired to join the Peoria Chapter of the Black Panther Party under his leadership.

Defense Captain Mark Clark's sister, Patricia was active in the Black Student Association at Illinois State University. She was in her senior year of college and played a role in organizing the April 1969 University Forum on Racism. Patricia escorted guest speaker, Reverend Jesse Jackson to the campus of Illinois State University in Normal, Illinois. Reverend Jackson was viewed by some African Americans as a potential successor to Dr. King; because of his work with SCLC Poor Peoples Campaign and Operation Breadbasket.

Dr. Patricia (Clark) Lewis

Prior to him taking the podium to speak, Patricia was among a group of over 200 black students who greeted him by raising their fists in the Black Power Salute. She was conscious of the revolutionary struggle her brother was engaged in and she understood the symbolism of her actions.

Later that same month, The Panther 21 were arrested in New York on conspiracy charges. Although none of them arrested had any recent or serious police record, bail was set at over $2 million. Among those arrested was Afeni Shakur (formerly Alice Williams) who was held on $100,000 bail.

The following month, on May 10, 1969 the Clark family was stunned by the sudden untimely death of Elder William Clark Sr. Elder Clark provided invaluable direction and support to his wife Mother Fannie Mae Clark and their seventeen children. He was Superintendent of Greater Central Illinois District of the Church of God in Christ, and President of the Interdenominational Ministers Alliance in the Greater Central Illinois District. He was Elder Pastor of Lincoln Avenue Church of God in Christ; and Founder of Holy Temple Church of God in Christ, both in Peoria. Elder Clark was employed by Caterpillar Tractor Company in East Peoria, Illinois where he worked twenty-eight years.

Defense Captain Mark Clark's father had no apparent illness at the time of his death. He was only 61 years old. One week before he died, he received the last of several anonymous letters in the mail. The last letter advised him that he didn't have long to live. Other anonymous letters came in the mail attempting to start a feud between Elder Clark and another Peoria Pastor. Members of Holy Temple COGIC held meetings prior to his death to get to the bottom of who was sending the anonymous letters. They never learned their actual origin, but over the years some members of the Clark family began to suspect that Elder William Clark Sr. was the victim of the FBI Counter Intelligence program launched against influential black religious and nationalist leaders.

When Defense Captain Mark Clark learned of their father's death, he gathered up several of his older brothers. They traveled to Illinois State University to get their sister Patricia and escort her back to Peoria. She had just received her college degree and was still in the dormitory. The Black Panther Party Leader, in his black leather jacket and black beret arrived with his brothers to console their sister and help her pack all her belongings. Before leaving Illinois State University, the Peoria Illinois Black Panther Party Leader spoke with college students on campus. He asked them to join in the struggle against racism and police brutality. He talked about the Black Panther

Party Ten-Point Program and the need for a proletarian revolution. Patricia recalled how the college students reacted. Seeing Mark with his brothers and sister left a definite impression. It struck Patricia how her younger brother had changed from a quiet young child to being an outspoken Black Panther Party Leader.

William Clark Sr. and Fannie Mae Clark

Mother Fannie Mae Clark grieved the loss of her beloved husband of almost forty years, and her best friend in life. Defense Captain Mark Clark grieved the loss of his beloved father along with the rest of his family, relatives, friends, and the church members. They were all deeply saddened by the death of a great man.

Elder William Clark, Sr. in his open coffin

Elder William Clark Sr. was the son of Alex Clark Sr. and Rena (Hullum) Clark. His Home Going Service was held on May 17, 1969 at Holy Temple Church of God in Christ in Peoria, Illinois where he was Elder Pastor and Founder. Bishop Eleazar Lenox of the Southern

Illinois Ecclesiastical Jurisdiction of the COGIC gave the Home Going eulogy. Elder William Clark Sr. was laid to rest in Springdale Cemetery in Peoria, Illinois.

After Elder Clark's interment, Mother Clark began to fear for the safety and security of her family. She no longer felt safe in Peoria, Illinois. She telephoned her cousin Riley Parks who lived in Flint, Michigan. When she talked to him he urged her to immediately come to Flint. She visited Flint and stayed with him for several days. During her visit, he contacted other relatives to see how they could assist in transitioning the Clark family to Flint. Fannie Mae Clark's cousin Kermit Brooks was among the relatives that migrated to Flint, Michigan from Macon, Mississippi. The Brooks moved into a new home on Oxley Drive in Flint. Cousin Kermit and his wife, Louise volunteered to help the family by renting Mother Clark their old home. During the summer of 1969, Defense Captain Mark Clark and several of his brothers helped their mother pack all her belongings. William Jr. drove their mother and the younger siblings to Flint. Fannie Mae Clark moved into her cousin Kermit's Florida Street home in the old Saint John's neighborhood near Buick City manufacturing plant.

Meanwhile, fearing the success of the Black Panthers Free Breakfast Program, Free People's Medical Clinic, and Political Education classes; the government set up a special task force to focus on eliminating the Black Panthers. Members of the Black Panther Party were maliciously charged with serious crimes; becoming political prisoners. Some were given lengthy prison sentences. Other Black Panthers were killed by police in cities and towns throughout the nation.

On May 26, 1969, as Chairman Fred Hampton Sr. sat in his jail cell awaiting sentencing for an alleged theft, he said "I have no life to give other than a life for the people. Let all tests of revolution confront me, those that I am not ready for, I will become ready for - People Unite". Several days later, on June 3, 1969 the Headquarters of the Chicago Chapter of the Black Panther Party was raided by the FBI. During the raid of the Chicago Chapter headquarters, they took money, membership lists, and literature. Although no fugitive was found, eight Panthers were arrested for harboring a fugitive.

By the end of July 1969, the police would totally destroy the Black Panther Party Headquarters in Chicago Illinois. Throughout the summer members of the Black Panther Party were arrested on attempted murder and other charges. Raids were conducted at other Black Panther Party Headquarters throughout the nation, including in Detroit, Denver, Sacramento, San Diego, and Los Angeles.

In September 1969, Mark Clark's oldest brother William Jr. drove back to Peoria to pick up several more siblings that were relocating to Flint, Michigan. Defense Captain Mark Clark asked his brother to drop him off in Chicago to meet with Chairman Fred Hampton Sr. When he exited his brother's car in Chicago, he had a premonition that he would be killed. He told his siblings to tell everybody he loved them because it would probably be the last time they see him alive. Several of his siblings attempted to convince him to come to Flint, Michigan. He would not abandon the Black Panther Party and Chairman Fred Hampton Sr. Defense Captain, Mark Clark was a man of honor and loyalty. He was a man who made a commitment to struggle for the people. Even in the face of overwhelming forces, he would not back down from his principles and values.

The FBI's COINTELPRO unit devised a plan to eliminate Chairman Fred Hampton, Sr. after deeming him a potential Black Messiah because of his influence. In order to obtain their objective, they conspired together with the U.S. Justice Department, Chicago Police Department, and Cook County States Attorney's Office. A raid was planned on the pretense that there were guns in Chairman Fred's 2337 West Monroe Street apartment on Chicago's south side. The real goal of the raid was to assassinate Chairman Fred Hampton Sr., and destroy the Black Panther Party.

FBI Agent Roy Mitchell met with informant William O'Neal who gave him a floorplan of the Monroe Street apartment to show where Chairman Fred was sleeping. He was paid $300 bonus for the floor plan and $17,000 for ongoing detailed information on the Chicago, Illinois Chapter of the Black Panther Party. The information he provided included detailed descriptions of Black Panther Party members and their daily routines. Agent Mitchell passed on all the information he received to a special racial matters unit. Richard Jolovec coordinated with Sergeant Daniel Groth and police officer James "Gloves" Davis, and the other policemen in the special police unit who would be responsible for carrying out the raid and assassinations.

The assassination plot to murder Chairman Fred Hampton Sr. most definitely included premeditation to murder Defense Captain Mark Clark. He was Chairman Fred's loyal Comrade in the Black Panther Party and a staunch revolutionary in the Black Power Liberation struggle. The Peoria, Illinois Black Panther Party Leader was dedicated to struggle and was not only a revolutionary in words but in deeds.

Chapter 8.

The December 4th Raid and Assassinations

The December 4th Raid and Assassinations

Chairman Fred Hampton Sr.
and Defense Captain Mark Clark

Early in the morning, December 4, 1969 there were nine members of the Black Panther Party asleep in the Monroe Street apartment of

Chairman Fred Hampton Sr. and his fiancée, Debra Johnson (now Akua Ngeri). The prior evening, FBI informant William O'Neal volunteered to make dinner for the Black Panthers. He spiked the Kool-Aid of Chairman Fred Hampton Sr. with secobarbital; a strong drug that induces unconsciousness. Afterwards, informant O'Neal left the apartment.

At approximately 4:45 am, the Cook County State Attorney; Edward Hanrahan initiated the gun raid. There were fourteen officers on the special squad. Eight officers entered at the front of the apartment, and six officers at the back. Police rushed inside the front of the apartment and began spraying the walls with gunfire. Their submachine guns penetrated the walls of Chairman Fred Hampton Sr. and his pregnant fiancée's bedroom.

Defense Captain Mark Clark was in the front living room asleep in a chair, when police forcibly kicked the door open and began shooting without warning. He was shot twice, once in the heart and once in the lung; and was killed instantly. According to Brenda Harris who watched from the bed across the room, Mark had a shotgun in his hand and his reflexes responded by firing one shot as he fell.

Chairman Fred Hampton Sr. was asleep in the back bedroom with his pregnant fiancée when he was shot in the shoulder from the submachine gunfire that penetrated through the wall. His pregnant fiancée, unable to wake him, was hurried out of the back bedroom into the kitchen. Several policemen enter the bedroom where they shot Chairman Fred several more times. Chairman Fred Hampton Sr. was shot a total of four times; twice in the head at point blank range. An officer was heard to have said "He's good and dead now". Police dragged Chairman Fred's dead body through the bedroom and out into the front room area; in a manner reminiscent of a trophy lynching.

Police continued to spray the apartment with submachine gun fire, entering from both the front and back doors of the apartment. Several Black Panthers were seriously wounded. Verlina Brewer and Ronald "Doc" Satchel were in the back bedroom with Blair Anderson when they were all injured. While in the living room with Louis Truelock and Harold Bell, Brenda Harris was shot twice by gun fire. The raid was described as lasting approximately 10 to 12 minutes; with 7 minutes of gunfire and 99 submachine gun shots fired by police.

After the police assassinated and seriously injured Black Panther Party members; several occupants were taken to the police station where they were threatened, assaulted, and battered. Several Black Panther raid survivors were charged with serious criminal offenses, including murder of police officers, attempted murder, and aggravated assault; resulting in their false imprisonment and malicious prosecution.

The funeral service for Chairman Fred Hampton Sr. was held on December 9th, 1969 at First Baptist Church in Melrose Park, Illinois. Five thousand people attended his funeral and passed by the open coffin as a sign of respect for the slain Black Panther Party Leader. After the funeral, Chairman Fred's body was taken to O'Hare National Airport to be transported to his family's ancestral hometown of Haynesville, Claiborne Parish, Louisiana. He was laid to rest in Bethel Cemetery.

The Clark family was devastated to learn the news of Mark Clark's brutal assassination by police. Mother Fannie Mae Clark was utterly dismayed how her son, Defense Captain Mark Clark and Chairman Fred were killed in the early morning hours as they slept. She questioned why police would want to destroy young black men with high ideals and the desire to end injustice in the community. The Clark's learned of Mark's death through a family friend that watched the TV news; and received no official notification from police.

When Mark Clark's siblings learned of his assassination, some cried out "look what they did, they killed my brother". Several siblings sat and consoled one another as they wept. Mark's youngest sister, Rose recalled how hurt she felt when she learned her brother had been murdered. She described how she cried and cried, and how her tears swelled even more each time she looked at her mother and other siblings. They were all heartbroken with grief. Mark's father, Elder Clark had just passed away months earlier and now they were dealing with the trauma of Mark's assassination. Rose wept constantly until her mother intervened and said "I don't want you to cry anymore for Mark; He just fulfilled his mission and God's got him now".

Mother Fannie Mae Clark began preparing for her son's funeral. She and the younger Clark children returned to Peoria from Flint, Michigan. Relatives of the family traveled from locations across the country. Mark Clark's brother James and his sister, Elner Clark traveled to Chicago to claim their brother's remains from the Cook County morgue. He was listed as an unknown person although police agencies and COINTELPRO were familiar with his background.

Mark Clark's body was transported from Chicago to his hometown Peoria, Illinois. Parks Funeral Home in Peoria was entrusted with the funeral and burial service. After personnel at the funeral home learned Mark Clark was a Black Panther Party Leader, they attempted to increase the price of funeral expenses. Members of the Black Panther Party stepped in and assisted the Clark family with the cost of Mark Clark's funeral and burial.

Funeral service for Defense Captain Mark Clark was held Saturday, December 13, 1969 at Freedom Hall in Peoria, Illinois. Hundreds of people attended the solemn funeral service. . Members of the Black Panther Party wore black leather jackets and black berets. They stood by in silent formation. Members of the Clark family passed the word to one another that they should not cry during the funeral service as a sign of respect for their brother's struggle in the Black Panther Party and his martyrdom. Mourners filed by Mark Clark's coffin as a sign of respect for the slain Defense Captain of the Black Panther Party and Peoria, Illinois Chapter Leader. Reverend Blaine Ramsey Jr. gave the eulogy.

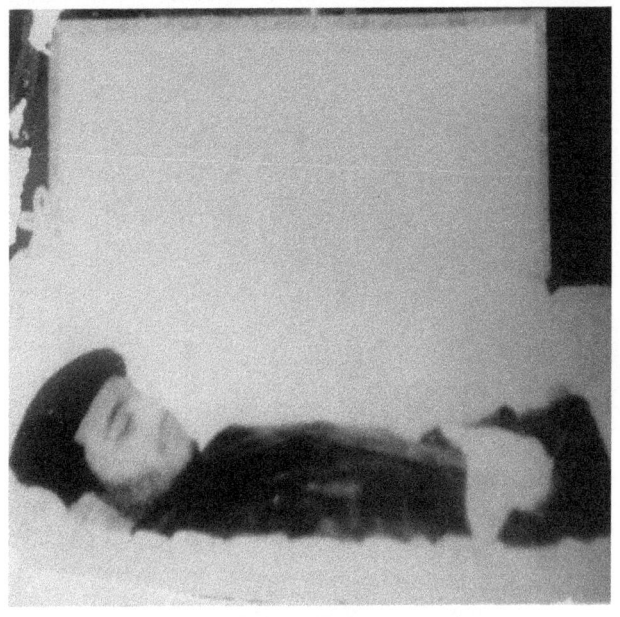

Mark Clark, Defense Captain of the Black Panther Party in his open coffin

Defense Captain Mark Clark was buried in black leather jacket and black beret, the aesthetics of the Black Panther Party. The Clark family wanted him buried as a Black Panther, symbolic of his revolutionary struggle. His burial was a testament to the nation and the world that Black Panther Mark Clark lived, worked, struggled, and died for the people. Mark Clark was the seventh son of Elder William and Fannie Mae Clark. His final resting place is Springdale Cemetery in Peoria, Illinois.

Matthew Clark (front), Charles Clark (in black beret) and mourners attending Defense Captain Mark Clark's burial service at Springdale Cemetery December 13, 1969

Chairman Bobby Seale of the Black Panther Party wrote from his jail cell in his book entitled, *Seize the Times: The Story of the Black Panther Party.* "Mark Clark and Chairman Fred Hampton, Sr. were among the group of African Americans demanding our constitutional rights, and demanding that our basic desires and needs be fulfilled, thus becoming the vanguard of a revolution, despite all attempts to totally wipe us out".

Chapter 9.

Media, Misinformation and Investigations

Media, Misinformation and Investigations

Many people were outraged by the assassinations of Black Panther Party Leaders, Chairman Fred Hampton Sr. and Defense Captain Mark Clark. Members of the Black Panther Party opened up the Monroe Street apartment to the community. In the cold winter, hundreds of concerned citizens stood in line outside the apartment; waiting to view the spray of submachine gun bullet holes. The Black Panther Party allowed the public to view for themselves the atrocities that had taken place there. When attorneys and law students from The Peoples Law Office learned that their client Chairman Fred Hampton, Sr. was murdered, they sent people to investigate what they saw at the Monroe Street apartment; and they helped preserve evidence.

Media outlets all over the country, including newspapers, television, and radio stations were putting out articles that distorted the truth, implicated the Black Panthers, and justified police actions. In an orchestrated effort, the Black Panthers were described as having guns and ammunitions, engaged in shootouts with police; and as thugs, hoodlums, troublemakers, and gang members. The Chicago Tribune article entitled *Panther Clark Expected Death Sister Reveals* was published in late December 1969. Mark Clark's sister, Elner Clark was interviewed by a reporter for the news story. The article he wrote appeared to twist her words and present a distorted image of who Mark Clark really was. Other newspapers such as The Peoria Journal Star seemed to focus on printing biased articles about the Black Panther Party as well.

The Cook County State's Attorney, Edward Hanrahan, spread knowingly false information in an effort to discredit the Black Panther Party members. Police claimed that Black Panthers were attempting to shoot police; and falsely claimed that they had confiscated 19 guns and 1000 rounds of ammunition from the Monroe Street apartment after the raid. The misinformation campaign consisted of outright lies, false evidence, conspiracy, and cover up. To hide the truth of the raid, police photographed guns and ammunition from another location and made it appear as if they were confiscated during the Black Panther raid. They took photographs of the back door of the apartment, which had several holes in it created by screws. They reported to media that the nail screw holes in the door came from gunshots fired by Black Panthers. They even produced a reenactment of events based on information they knew to be false.

The police claims would later be disproved by expert examination, witness testimony, and documents presented into evidence in various court proceedings. Once the autopsy report of Chairman Fred Hampton Sr. was released, it brought into question the police's account of his death. The results of the autopsy report showed that Fred Hampton Sr. was asleep at the time of his death; and was under the effects of secobarbital, which rendered him unconscious. These findings led members of the community to call for a review by an independent commission to look into whether the police violated the Black Panthers civil rights.

In response to many concerns voiced by the community and local congressional leaders, the City of Chicago held a Coroner's Blue Ribbon Panel Inquest on January 6, 1970.

Mother Fannie Mae Clark and several other Clark family members attended the inquest. Mother Clark was furious with the decision of the Coroner's Inquest Jury. She adamantly proclaimed, "It's not right, it's just not right"! The inquest was headed by a specially appointed Deputy Coroner, Martin S. Gerber. After only 12 days and five hours of deliberation a six-man Blue Ribbon Coroner's Jury returned a verdict of justifiable homicide in the deaths of Mark and Fred. An attorney for the Black Panthers described the inquest as orchestrated to vindicate the police officers. All criminal charges against the police in the raid were dismissed.

That same month, a State Grand Jury indicted several of the surviving Black Panthers on attempted murder and other charges. Later, a Federal Grand Jury determined that police fired between 82 and 99 shots while most of the occupants lay asleep. The Federal Grand Jury determined that only one shot was proven to have come from a Black Panther Party member's gun. It was further noted that the State's Attorney's Office was a partner to the conspiracy, and as such had a conflict of interest in their indictment of Black Panther survivors in the raid. Eventually, all charges against the Black Panther survivors were dropped.

However, charges against the police were dismissed as well. In early 1970, Fannie Mae Clark, Iberia Hampton, and Black Panther raid survivors filed lawsuits. The lawsuits were filed against the City of Chicago, Cook County, and Cook County State's Attorney, Edward Hanrahan. Fannie Mae Clark filed a wrongful death lawsuit on behalf of her son, Defense Captain, Mark Clark. Initially, she selected the NAACP's Christopher O'Toole as her lead attorney. He was assisted by NAACP's James Montgomery, The American Civil Liberties Union and The People's Law Office, including Attorney Jeffrey Haas, Flint Taylor, and other lawyers and law students. Eventually, Fannie Mae Clark would select the young lawyers of The People's Law Office to be her lead attorneys.

When Ebony and Jet Magazines learned that the families of the assassinated Black Panthers were filing lawsuits; they wrote several articles. Fannie Mae Clark spoke several times with black media outlets and told them why she filed the lawsuit. Her statements were in Jet Magazine's October 15, 1970 issue; along with photographs of Mark Clark and Fred Hampton. In the Jet article, Fannie Mae Clark talked about the police's use of excessive and indiscriminant force. She spoke of how the police denied her son his constitutional rights. Fannie Mae Clark told the magazine that she wanted to "right a wrong". The article also mentioned that her daughter, Ella Mae (Clark) Marion recently passed away of a heart attack. She was the first child born to Elder William and Fannie Mae Clark. She passed away in September 1970. Her death was the fourth to occur in the Clark family since 1968. She was only 37 years old at the time of her death. Ella Mae was a beloved wife and mother. The entire Clark family, including her two sons, Daryl and Craig Marion grieved her sudden and tragic loss. Her final resting place is Springdale Cemetery in Peoria, Illinois.

The Clark family experienced major grief after the untimely deaths of Defense Captain Mark Clark, Elder William Clark Sr., Ella Bardley, and Ella Mae (Clark) Marion. Adding to the family's trauma was the government's apparent focus on other members of the Clark family. The Clark's telephones were wire-tapped and their since of privacy and security lost as the government listened in on personal conversations and monitored family members. Police took one of Mark's younger brothers to the Peoria jail where he was shown photographs of the younger members of the family in an effort to intimidate him. The threats, wire-tapping, and surveillance were tactics designed to create trauma and instill fear. The Clark family was determined not to let those tactics mentally enslave them.

The 1969 assassinations of Chairman Fred Hampton Sr. and Defense Captain Mark Clark, and the police brutality perpetrated on the Black Panther Party raid survivors affected African Americans all across the nation. Chairman Fred Hampton Sr. and Peoria, Illinois Chapter Leader Mark Clark inspired many people who did not want their struggle to be in vain. The Clark family received support from people across the nation who encouraged Mother Clark in her fight for justice.

In 1970, the Black Panther Party was at its height of membership. Comrades in Black Panther Party Chapters and activists in community organizations across the nation worked to get streets renamed in honor of Black Panther Party Leader, Chairman Fred Hampton Sr. In February 1971, the Black Panther Party Newspaper printed an article entitled *Brotherly Love Can Kill You.* The article described the

Mark Clark People's Free Medical Clinic in Philadelphia, Pennsylvania. The clinic served thousands and provided sickle cell anemia testing. The Clark family was deeply moved to learn that the People's Free Medical Clinic in Philadelphia was named in honor of Mark Clark.

During the 1970's, there was no longer coordination among religious groups, black activists, and Black Power Liberation groups. No longer were there mass protests or boycotting. The Civil Rights Movement was over. As the decade of the 1970's progressed, members of the Black Panther Party continued struggling against racism and injustice. The Black Panthers worked to establish community health centers and community-based economic programs. They continued to be targets of the FBI COINTELPRO and police actions. Black Panthers were wrongfully charged with criminal offenses. Some were given lengthy prison sentences; and others were killed. Eventually, membership in the organization declined as the tide of revolution was chilled.

Chapter 10

Thirteen Years of Trials and Appeals

Thirteen Years of Trials and Appeals

The Clark and Hampton families and Black Panther Party raid survivors were plaintiffs in the civil rights lawsuits brought before the U.S. District Court. It would take two civil trials, two Seventh Circuit Court of Appeal decisions, a Supreme Court ruling, and various other court proceedings; all resulting in a 13-year battle in the courts.

The first trial began in U.S. District Court in October 1971, in the courtroom of Judge Joseph Samuel Perry. The Judge combined the various plaintiff lawsuits into the class action lawsuit known as Hampton v Hanrahan. Clark and Hampton families, and other Black Panther survivors were assisted by attorneys from The Peoples Law Office; NAACP, and American Civil Liberties Union.

Fannie Mae Clark and several of her children traveled from Flint, Michigan for each of the court proceedings. Her daughter, Dr. Patricia (Clark) Lewis accompanied her to court throughout the first trial. Patricia recalled the tension in the courtroom. She watched the expressions on the police officer's faces who actually initiated and carried out the raid. She wanted to see if they would show some type of remorse for their actions, especially police officer James "Gloves". Davis. He was the African American officer who was responsible for firing submachine gun shots into both Mark Clark and Fred Hampton, Sr. He was known in the community as an infamous Chicago cop who often exhibited brutality. None of the police officers ever looked remorseful and they stuck to their story claiming that the raid was justified. Without glaring evidence of conspiracy, there was essentially no way the Judge would allow the case to proceed. By February 1972, the trial ended when the case was dismissed by Judge Perry. Charges against States Attorney Edward Hanrahan and co-defendant police were all dismissed.

By early 1973, the Commission of Inquiry introduced its findings about the December 4th, 1969 Black Panther Party raid. The commission report was prepared by NAACP's Roy Wilkens and Ramsey Clark, former U.S. Attorneys General. The report was entitled: *Search and Destroy: A Report by the Commission of Inquiry into the Black Panthers and the Police.* The report described police efforts to destroy the Black Panthers and the government's use of misinformation. The common theme throughout the report was that the government failed to see the Black Panthers as full and equal human beings.

Meanwhile, plaintiff lawyers appealed Judge Perry's decision to dismiss the case in the first trial. The appeal was heard in the Seventh Circuit Court of Appeals. During the appeal, the testimony of various witnesses during the District Court trial was scrutinized. The appeals court reviewed the testimony of experts and conflicting testimony given by government witnesses and Black Panther raid survivors. .For instance, the autopsy performed on Mark Clark showed that he was killed instantly, while in the chair. The police alleged that Mark was shooting at them when he was murdered. The Appeals Court looked at the testimony of Black Panther raid survivors regarding these discrepancies.

Black Panther raid survivor Brenda Harris was among those in the living room when Mark Clark was killed. She testified that Mark was holding a shotgun and shooting, as police were claiming. Another Black Panther raid survivor later provided a sworn statement to the court that another Black Panther was shooting as well. This information led to questions and concerns. Why would members of the Black Panther Party testify and/or sign sworn statements that other Black Panther Party members were shooting at police?

Fannie Mae Clark, Patricia (Clark) Lewis and Calvin Lewis Sr. speak out at trial.

The Appeals Court discussed Fannie Mae Clark's complaint of her son's wrongful death. The complaint read, "Officers shot and killed Mark Clark without any authority of law; and thereby denied him due process of law by imposing summary punishment of death upon him" Eventually, the Black Panther plaintiffs and their attorneys won the appeal; and the court remanded the case back to the U.S. District Court; requiring a new 2nd trial.

In the wake of the Watergate scandal, Senator Frank Church's Select Committee to Study Governmental Operations (Church Committee) was investigating various abuses by the FBI and intelligence agencies. An attorney affiliated with the committee informed Black Panther Party attorneys about secret documents. This tip eventually helped them link the assassinations of Chairman Fred Hampton Sr. and Defense Captain Mark Clark to the FBI COINTELPRO.

The 2nd trial began January 1976 in U.S. District Court; presided over by Judge Sam Perry; which was the same Judge that dismissed the first trial. During the trial's initial discovery process, the government produced only 34 documents. However, testimony of the government's own witnesses clearly revealed more documents existed. Little by little additional documents were handed over to Black Panthers attorneys: and each time exposing more of the conspiracy and cover-up between FBI, justice department and police. Eventually, the Judge ordered all the files pertaining to the raid to be turned over.

On the last day of the 2nd trial, the jury deliberated but was unable to reach a unanimous verdict. Judge Perry then ruled unilaterally to dismiss the case and all charges against defendants. Black Panther Party lawyers objected to the unilateral dismissal, which made Judge Perry become even more hostile. The Judge told Black Panther lawyers to shut up repeatedly. Judge Perry was clearly not going to allow the Black Panther Party plaintiffs to receive a fair trial in his courtroom. The Judge even went so far as to cite several attorneys for contempt of court. The Judge's apparent prejudice and hostility against the Black Panther plaintiffs and lawyers showed they would not receive justice.

By the time the 2nd trial ended, Black Panther lawyers had identified 213 documents to admit as evidence, (instead of the 34 initially produced by the government). The government's failure to abide by fair process of discovery and disclosure of documents was a clear violation of civil rights. The trial was on record as lasting as the longest in U.S. Federal District Court history at that time, starting January 1976 until May 1977.

On August 14, 1978 attorney's representing the Black Panthers argued again to the Seventh Circuit Court of Appeals Judges Fairchild, Wygert, and Pell. This time they were seeking to overturn Judge Perry's unilateral decision to dismiss all charges in the 2nd trial. During the 2nd appeal, Black Panther's lawyers amended the lawsuit based on discovery of FBI COINTELPRO involvement; adding four federal defendants from the FBI Racial Matters squad. On April 23, 1979 Black Panther lawyers and plaintiffs won the 2nd appeal.

The Seventh Circuit Court of Appeals ruled that the government sought to discredit the Black Panthers, disrupt the breakfast program for children, promote violent conflicts, and encourage dissension. Many other troubling facts came to light during the appeal, including that the raid was designed to neutralize the

Black Panthers. The appeals court found that government officials engaged in a subsequent cover-up to conceal the true nature of the raid, harass the survivors, and frustrate any legal redress. The Seventh Circuit Court of Appeals said that government lawyers obstructed justice by failing to turn over documents necessary to receive a fair trial. In doing so, they violated Black Panther Party member's civil rights; thereby depriving them of their constitutional rights under the 14th amendment. Finally, the appeals court said the case should have been allowed to be determined by the jury; instead of a unilateral ruling from Judge Perry in the 2nd trial.

After the 2nd appeal ended, the justice department acted quickly to give qualified immunity to the FBI agents involved in the Black Panther Party raid so they would not be subjected to prosecution. Chicago police and Cook County continued to request hearings on immunity; but the justice department refused to hold additional hearings. The government continued to fight the appeals court rulings and sought to have the Seventh Circuit Court of Appeals opinion reversed in the U.S. Supreme

Court. The Supreme Court, in a vote of 5-3 refused to overturn the decision of the Seventh Circuit Court of Appeals.

In late 1982, the case Hampton v. Hanrahan was remanded back to U.S. District court again; awaiting a 3rd trial. This time the case was not assigned to Judge Perry because he had been sanctioned for various actions he took during and after the trials. The government placed strict limits on his case load. The new Judge assigned to the case indicated that he might impose severe Sanctions against the government defendants. However, in February 1983 the U.S. government, Cook County, and City of Chicago agreed to settle the lawsuit for 1.85 million dollars. The monetary amounts were divided between the families of Hampton, Clark, Black Panther raid survivors, and the attorneys.

The extent of the government's infiltration of the Black Panther Party may never be known. The FBI's COINTELPRO conspiracy, planning of the December 4th raid, the government's subsequent cover-up, and the conflicting testimony of witnesses during trials leave many questions and concerns. Among them is whether the Black Panthers ever shot weapons at all. No forensic evidence was ever obtained to show it; and court documents later revealed there was only one bullet found to have been linked to a Panther's gun. Only one weapon was found in the Monroe Street apartment; and it was a legally purchased handgun. The entire conspiracy leaves a person to wonder whether there were additional informants in the Chicago Chapter of the Black Panther Party who remained covert.

Chapter 11

Clark Family Values and Moving Forward

The Clark Family Values and Moving Forward

By the early 1980's, the Black Panther Party organization dissolved. Instead of active engagement in ending racism and injustice; many black people were lulled into passivity by television, movies, and music. TV Shows like *Sanford and Son* and *Good Times* were widely popular among African Americans. These shows conveyed messages that living in the projects was a "good time" and owning a junk yard wasn't monetarily beneficial.

Black Exploitation films like *Superfly* and *Foxy Brown* came to the big screen. These films conveyed romanticized stereotypical characters of drug dealers, pimps, prostitutes, and private eye detectives. Mark Clark's brother, Matthew relocated to Los Angeles, California where he played a gangster in comedian Richard Pryor's 1980's films, *Bustin Loose* and *Some Kind of Hero*.

Matthew Clark
(Also shown with Richard Pryor
in movie scene from *Bustin Loose)*

In 1983, after the longest trial in U.S. District Court history and the publicity of the lawsuit; Mother Fannie Mae Clark was concerned for the safety of her children. She prayed as she always did, saying "God help me and my children". As she awoke one morning, she heard an audible voice in her ear saying "There is safety in the ark". When she opened her newspaper that day, she was led to look in the classified section where she saw a church building for sale. She hurried to tell her son, Minister William Clark Jr.; and they both went to take a look at the church building. At such a reduced price, she purchased the building immediately. The new church was named the Ark of Safety Church of God in Christ.

The Ark of Safety Church of God in Christ was founded in 1983 in Flint, Michigan. The church Pastor was Minister William Clark Jr. The pastors' wife led the testimony service which usually began by singing the song, *Talk About Jesus*. Minister Clark would sometimes run up and down the isles as he worshiped God. There were dedicated church members like Mother Jones who the congregation loved to see activate the church. She had many animated performances on the piano. Mother Clark enjoyed praising God and playing the tambourine. The church was set up in a manner that when someone happened to come in late, everyone would look back and see who came in. The congregation was made up of mostly relatives and close friends. The Clark family looked forward to seeing each other there. Mother Fannie Mae Clark found peace of mind in the Ark of Safety Church of God in Christ.

The Ark of Safety COGIC congregation loved to fellowship with other churches. Among the visiting congregations was Pentecostal Compassion Church of God in Christ. Before the founding of the Ark of Safety COGIC, Mother Clark and her children attended Pentecostal Compassion regularly. Pentecostal Compassion COGIC was founded in the 1970's by Elder Lonnie Royster Sr. and his wife, Evangelist Mother Geneva Royster. Mother Clark and Mother Royster were both powerful prayer warriors and women of similarly sweet spirits. They were like mother and daughter and often went shopping together to find bargains for their numerous family members. The Ark of Safety Church of God in Christ and Pentecostal

Compassion COGIC fellowshipped together in love and unity.

Mother Fannie Mae Clark and her children would fellowship at churches throughout Flint, Michigan. When she first arrived in Flint, she was welcomed by Pastor, Bishop Fred Lewis and his family. Mother Clark fellowshipped with the congregation at Hamilton Avenue COGIC and was close friends with Missionary Louise Gates. Other churches which were beloved to her were Faith Gospel Temple COGIC, Pastor, Superintendent Elder J. E. Walker Sr.; Deliverance COGIC, Pastor Zach Smith Sr.; Civic Heights COGIC, Pastor Samuel Marsh Sr.; and Greater Holy Temple COGIC, Bishop Roger Jones.

Since 1935, Mother Fannie Mae Clark attended the Holy Convocation of the COGIC in Memphis. It was one of her great pleasures. She talked about how friendly and neighborly they were in Memphis and how people you never met before would address you by saying, "Praise the Lord Saint". Whenever she made the trip, she was sure to bring several of her beautiful hats which she kept neatly in her special hat boxes. Hats were symbolic of her spiritual covering and a special part of her church tradition.

Mother Fannie Mae Clark sitting in a Wicker Chair at the International Holy Convocation of the COGIC in Memphis, Tennessee

Mother Clark loved to hear the Saints sing and shout. She felt the power of the multitude whenever she entered Mason Temple. In the 1980's, she attended the International Holy Convocation under the leadership of COGIC's Presiding Bishop J. O. Paterson, Sr. In the 1990's, Illinois Bishop Louis H. Ford became the Presiding Bishop of the COGIC. Mother Clark was so glad when Bishop Ford became Presiding Bishop. Her late husband, Elder William Clark Sr. served as Superintendent of the Greater Central Illinois District of the COGIC under Bishop Eleazar Lenox and Bishop Louis H. Ford.

When Mother Clark was not attending church, she was spending quality time with family. She sponsored many events to bring the entire family together in a spirit of love, unity, and thanksgiving. Clark Family Reunions were held regularly. The reunions included remembrances and candlelight ceremonies recognizing the ancestors. Reunions were typically held in Peoria, Illinois but over the years they took place in locations such as Flint, Michigan and Atlanta, Georgia. Clark Family Reunions were attended by relatives from all over the nation.

Mother Fannie Mae Clark was a professional Cake Decorator. She made a Cake for every occasion, including The Clark Family Reunions.

Elder William Clark's sister, Irene (Clark) Howard attended many of the Clark family Reunions with her children and grandchildren. Aunt Irene usually led the Clark family in prayer and singing. Everyone gathered around holding hands as she led the family prayer and singing old-time gospel songs like *Wade in the Water*.. Elder Clark's siblings, Anna Lee (Clark) Mabry and Alex Clark Jr. maintained close connectivity with the family; and they attended during the earlier years. Their children and grandchildren continued to attend the Clark Family Reunions years later. Mother Clark's Aunt Lillie Mae and her daughter, Adelle (Williams) Gordon attended most of the Clark Family Reunions.. The Williams, Gordons and all their children and grandchildren attended faithfully over the years.

Mother Clark's cousin, Riley Parks usually attended the Clark Family Reunion in Flint, Michigan. Every now and then he would attempt to explain how the ancestors ended up in Mississippi. With his deep southern draw, he said "Now ya see, there was two sisters that came from Vergini and they married two brothers, and that's how we became kinfolk". Cousin Riley's information led several family members to conduct ancestry research. While combing through census records and historical information, Fannie Mae Clark's youngest daughter, Rose found records dating back to the 1870's, when their Great grandmother, Fannie Brewer was born. Census records indicated that

Fannie Brewer's parents were enslaved. The Clark's great, great grandmother, Melinda Brewer was born in Mississippi in 1843. Her mother came from the State of Virginia. This supported Cousin Riley's account of events.

2016 Clark Family Reunion
Ancestry Presentation

Rose shared her findings during the 2016 Clark Family Reunion, in Peoria, Illinois. Her presentation was entitled *Together We Are A Family*. The presentation covered the ancestors journey from Virginia to the prairie lands of Mississippi and Alabama around the 1820's. More than 50 family surnames were identified; each an ancestral branch which emerged. The Clark Family Reunions were forums where they shared their experiences and talked about their family history.

Elner (McNeese) Partlow Blackburn was among the relative that attended the Clark Family Reunions. She was Fannie Mae Clark's aunt whom the family affectionately called Aintee. Her first husband was lynched years earlier in Mississippi. His lynching affected how Aintee interacted with people. Even when she was well beyond 70 years old, she still bragged about carrying a gun. She talked about how well she could fight and knock a person upside their head. Fannie Mae Clark knew just what to say in response to Aintee's tough talk but she always showed her genuine affection and the utmost respect; and made sure the Clark children respected her too.

The lynching of Aintee's husband, the assassinations of numerous Civil Rights Leaders, Black Nationalist and revolutionaries such as Black Panther Party Leaders, Defense

Captain Mark Clark and Chairman Fred Hampton Sr., as well as the ongoing atrocities committed against countless black people on an ongoing basis is all part of a systematic plan of oppression. Among the tactics used by the oppressor is trauma and fear designed to immobilize and neutralize.

When the United States government assassinated Mark Clark, it traumatized the entire Clark family. Despite the trauma and fear, Fannie Mae Clark took action. She spoke out against the police's use of excessive and indiscriminant force and fought back in the legal system over thirteen years. Ultimately, she received a lawsuit settlement but the perpetrators of her son's assassination were never found criminally responsible.

After all the legal proceedings, Fannie Mae Clark tried to put the devastating assassinations and the turbulent times behind her. Well in her sixties, she returned to school at Beecher Adult High School in Flint, Michigan. She received her High School Equivalence by GED which was a feat she desired to accomplish since receiving an 8th grade education in Mississippi. She received one of the highest scoring grades in her class. She attributed her high GED score to her love of reading, writing, and the numerous encyclopedias which she studied over the years.

Many of Mark Clark's siblings worked to improve social and economic conditions. Elner Clark worked with the locally organized United Front in Peoria to restart the Free Breakfast Program. Samuel Clark worked toward social change within the local educational system in Flint, Michigan. Seeing that school children in Flint were required to pay for bus transportation, he lodged a complaint with the Flint School Board in protest stating that "to pay to go to school was against the constitution, as the fee denied students the right to a public education". After numerous public hearings, he was successful in having the bus transportation fee eliminated permanently. James Clark established various memorials and tributes to commemorate Mark Clark and the Black Panthers; and he continued to speak out against their assassinations.

Several of Mark's siblings made significant contributions in Business and Education; working towards social change within their chosen fields. Dr. Patricia (Clark) Lewis opened the first Charter School in Clayton County, Georgia. Rose (Clark) Morris worked toward improving economic opportunities, housing, education, and healthcare in the Human Resources field.

Although the family moved forward, they will never forget the atrocities of the December 4th raid and assassinations of Black Panther Party Leaders, Defense Captain Mark Clark and Chairman Fred Hampton, Sr.

Despite the remarkable history of the Black Panther Party, its role in the Civil Rights Movement was paid little attention by the mainstream movie industry until the mid-1990's. In 1995, Mario Van Peebles directed the movie *Panther*. His film sought to inspire and educate the current generation about the Black Panther Party. The film portrayed many facets of the Black Panthers, although it omitted the infamous December 4th raid and assassinations. Members of the Clark family attended the movie during its opening at the Showcase Cinemas in Flint, Michigan.

Photo of Mark Clark in Flint Journal Newspaper and Kay Clark and Jaclyn (Clark) Hodge shown at Premiere of movie *Panther*.

After its viewing, several Clark family members were interviewed by a reporter from the Flint Journal Newspaper. Mark Clark's sister. Kay shared with the newspaper reporter how her brother started the free breakfast program in Peoria. The youngest of Mark Clark's siblings, Rose (Clark) Morris talked about how the Black Panther Party stressed self-help, discipline and empowerment, not racism. Fannie Mae Clark told the newspaper reporter about how people were describing the Black Panthers as being instigators, haters, and anti-religion, and she said of her son, "Mark was a Sunday School Boy".

Soon after giving the interview to the Flint Journal Newspaper, Fannie Mae Clark decided that it was time for her to go back to Peoria, Illinois where she lived almost thirty years, prior to coming to Flint in 1969. She was 81 years old at the time she moved back to Peoria. Upon her return, she reunited with the congregation at Holy Temple Church of God in Christ where her husband, the late Elder William Clark, Sr. was Founder.

Chronicle of the Seventh Son
Black Panther Mark Clark

Chapter 12

Memorials, Tributes and Love Letters

Memorials, Tributes and Love Letters

Near the end of the 20th century came the death of several Clark family members. In September 1993, Minister William Clark Jr. passed away in Flint, Michigan. He was the second child born to Elder William and Fannie Mae Clark. He was a husband and father. He was Pastor of Ark of Safety Church of God in Christ in Flint, Michigan. He was a Veteran of the U.S. Army serving 12 years during the Korean and Vietnam Wars. His final resting place is Flint Memorial Park Cemetery in Mt. Morris, Michigan.

Joseph Clark passed away in November 1995. He was the twelfth child born to Elder William and Fannie Mae Clark. He was a husband and father. He enjoyed playing and watching sports, especially basketball and football; and was only 41 years old when he passed away. His final resting place is Gracelawn Cemetery in Flint, Michigan.

Mother Fannie Mae Clark passed away in August 1998 in Peoria, Illinois. She was a beloved mother, Missionary, Evangelist, Story Teller, and Poet. She was a praying woman who diligently carried out her work and responsibilities.

Mother Fannie Mae Clark

Mother Fannie Mae Clark spoke of a dream she had after her husband, the late Elder William Clark Sr. passed away in 1969. In her dream she died too. Two angels were at her bedside ready to take her over to the other side of the river; and she was concerned for the welfare of her children. She asked one of the angels, "What will my children do without me?" The angel replied, "We'll have to see what the man on the other side of the river says". The two angels took her by her hands and feet to carry her to the other side of the river but before they got there another angel met them and said "Take Her Back!" At that very moment, her daughter Patricia, hearing her moaning in bed came and awakened her. Years later, Mother Clark would talk about that dream and she would proclaim "I was blessed not only to see my children grown; but my children's, children's; children." Mother Fannie Mae Clark was truly blessed and she lived many more years after her husband's death.

During Mother Clark's life she sponsored many family gatherings. Some gatherings were planned and others were impromptu. Each gathering was for the purpose of allowing her large family circle to enjoy one another. She often reminded her children to telephone or visit relatives and she encouraged them to maintain close connectivity with each other. Her youngest daughter, Rose described her beloved mother saying, "Momma was a beautiful spirit and she loved to laugh and commune with all her friends and loved ones". "She was a woman favored of God and just like King David in the Bible; she once slew a giant too". The civil rights lawsuit filed by Fannie Mae Clark in the death of her son Mark Clark, and other plaintiffs led to the uncovering of documents implicating the government's involvement in the Black Panther Leaders assassinations. Her lawsuit exposed a covert program known as COINTELPRO.

Mother Fannie Mae Clark was the daughter of Samuel and Ella (Terrell) Bardley. She was 84 years old when she passed away. Her Home Going Service was held at Holy Temple Church of God in Christ in Peoria, Illinois. Bishop John Cobb gave the eulogy. Mother Fannie Mae Clark's final resting place is Parkview Cemetery in Peoria, Illinois.

Charles Clark was the seventh child born to Elder William and Fannie Mae Clark. He passed away in February 2002. He was a husband and father. He loved to laugh, attend Black Arts Festivals, recite poetry, and travel to churches to play his saxophone. Charles attended Illinois Central College and Xavier College. His final resting place is Parkview Cemetery in Peoria, Illinois.

James Clark

The Mark Clark Memorial Foundation was established in 2008 by Clark family members. The foundation originators were George Clark, Board President; James Clark,

Board Chairman; Elner Clark, Board Vice-President; and Kay Clark, Board Secretary. The foundation held its first Mark Clark Memorial Tribute at Carver Community Center in Peoria, Illinois on June 28th, 2008. The event was held in commemoration of Mark Clark's birthday. Guest speakers for the Tribute were Attorney Flint Taylor of The People's Law Office and Professor, Dr. Charles Jones, African American Studies Department Chair at Georgia State University and author of the book entitled, *The Black Panthers Reconsidered.*

A group of artists and activists known as BASE created the "From the Root" project. They erected billboards in public spaces to honor those who struggled for freedom. The project erected several billboards to honor Chairman Fred Hampton Sr. and Defense Captain Mark Clark. A billboard was installed at 2344 West Madison Street in Chicago, Illinois; directly across from the original spot where the Black Panther Party Headquarters was located. The other billboard was installed at 2337 West Monroe Street, the site of the December 4th 1969 raid and assassinations. The Mark Clark Memorial Foundation held its second Memorial Tribute to Mark Clark on June 27, 2009 at Lovejoy Church in Peoria, Illinois.

The following December, members of the Clark family attended the 40th Anniversary Ceremonies of the December 4th Raid held in Chicago, Illinois on December 4, 2009. Clark family members were among those gathered at the Monroe Street apartment to commemorate the lives of the slain Black Panther Party Leaders, Chairman Fred Hampton Sr., Defense Captain Mark Clark, and the other Black Panther raid survivors.

Among the program speakers were Chairman Fred Hampton, Jr., son of Chairman Fred Hampton Sr. Chairman Fred Jr. is Leader of the Black Panther Party Cubs and he is the *Free Em All* Talk Radio Host. His mother, Akua Njeri (formerly Debra Johnson), was the fiancée of Chairman Fred Hampton Sr. and Black Panther Party raid survivor. She was 8 ½ months pregnant with Chairman Fred Jr. at the time of the raid. Also speaking at the event was James Clark, the brother of Mark Clark and Chairman of the Mark Clark Memorial Foundation.

In Commemoration of the 40th Anniversary Matthew Clark wrote a letter of poetry.

LETTER TO A PANTHER

My Dear Brother,

It's after midnight and my house is quiet. Outside the Santa Ana winds are raging at almost 70 miles per hour. My computer is near the window, giving me a clear view of the violent force of nature as it bends and shakes the trees. Occasionally the swirling winds slams directly against my window pane, rattling the vertical blinds. Then, suddenly the winds calm.

Mark, your change was sudden as the Santa Ana winds. You were like Moses coming down from the mountain; however, it was the Ten Point Program from the Black Panther Party Platform you held in your hand.

You said you finally understood that your youth and strength was not your own to squander. You said your purpose was to protect the weak members of the community. So you set up a breakfast program for children, rescued jaded girls from their pimps, and provided support and transportation for seniors. "All power to the people!"

Mark! You have become a man, but you were not a father. You would never be a father because the beast was loose and already on your scent. While I lay in my cell that December night, the smell of blood was filling the nostrils of the beast. It was the smell of Panther blood. It was the smell of your blood.

Remember when my greatest ambition was to be a magician? When I told you the flame would not burn, you held out your hand without flinching. I didn't think I was being mean to you. In my distorted thinking I was training you. I was preparing you for life and death situations. Then, when that situation materialized, I wasn't there.

I was escorted home for your funeral, but I didn't cry for you. I was so happy just to be outside the wall. When I saw each family member as they lined up to march into the church, I was happy again, and again. Then word was passed along the line, "No tears! Don't cry! Don't let them see you cry!"

When our mother led your sixteen remaining siblings into the church, each jaw was firmly set, every eye was dry, and on each face the firm resolution was apparent. "Don't let — them-see-you cry!"

I set here at my computer, and suddenly without warning they come. Tears held back for forty years They rise up from deep inside me to mingle with the sounds of the wind against my windowpane and the jangling sounds of the vertical blinds. I don't hold back. I let them flow. For, they are not tears for an injustice done, nor tears for a Panther slain. They are tears for you, Mark; the little brother that I miss.

Your Brother, Matt

George Clark passed away in December 2009. He was the sixth child born to Elder William and Fannie Mae Clark. He was a husband and father. Prior to his death, he was Board President of the Mark Clark Memorial Foundation. He was a U.S. Army Veteran serving two terms of active military duty as a Military Policeman in the Korean and Vietnam Wars. He was awarded the National Defense Medal, Marksman Badge, and Good Conduct Medal. His final resting place is Springdale Cemetery in Peoria, Illinois.

Kay Clark passed away in June 2011. She was the thirteenth child born to William and Fannie Mae Clark. She was an Administrative Assistant for many years and worked for several prominent companies. Prior to her death, she was the Board Secretary for the Mark Clark Memorial Foundation. Her final resting place is River Rest Cemetery in Flint, Michigan.

Samuel Clark passed away in September 2013. He was the third child born to Elder William and Fannie Mae Clark. He was a husband and father. He was a U.S. Army Veteran of the Korean War; serving in Germany in the Tank Battalion. His final resting place is Great Lakes National Cemetery in Holly, Michigan.

James Clark was the fourth child born to Elder William and Fannie Mae Clark. He passed away in May 2015. James was a husband and father. He was a smart legal mind and an excellent orator. Prior to his death, he was the Board Chairman for the Mark Clark Memorial Foundation. He worked to establish memorials in various cities in commemoration of his brother, Mark Clark. He collected memorabilia which he used to educate the public.

James confessed years ago to serious criminal offenses against police while attempting to avenge his brother's death. He provided a signed confession to police officials for crimes he committed and he tried to make amends for his pass misdeeds. James joined the Ark of Safety COGIC under the leadership of his brother, Minister William Clark Jr. Eventually, James was called into ministry and became Pastor of Holiness is the Way Church in Flint, Michigan. His final resting place is River Rest Cemetery in Flint, Michigan.

Mark Clark, Defense Captain of the Black Panther Party and Peoria Illinois Chapter Leader was inducted into the Peoria Afro American Hall of Fame in 2011. The following year his photograph was placed in the Peoria Riverfront Museum in commemoration of his role in the Black Panther Party. His legacy will forever be his revolutionary activism.

Mark Clark was a revolutionary with a heightened awareness of injustice. He spent the last seven years of his life fighting against it. He began standing up against injustice when he was fifteen years old. His activism in the NAACP was protesting and boycotting for civil rights. His ability to influence youth in Peoria led to increased participation in sit-ins and boycotts. He was instrumental in the success of the Peoria Bus Boycott of 1963 and the sit-ins and demonstrations in Peoria during Freedom Summer of 1964. His activism led to demands being met and civil rights successes in the 1960's.

Mark exhibited the courage and tenacity to take a stand against the Capitalist structure. He understood the need for the people to unite against injustice. Mark Clark was not just a revolutionary in words, but deeds.

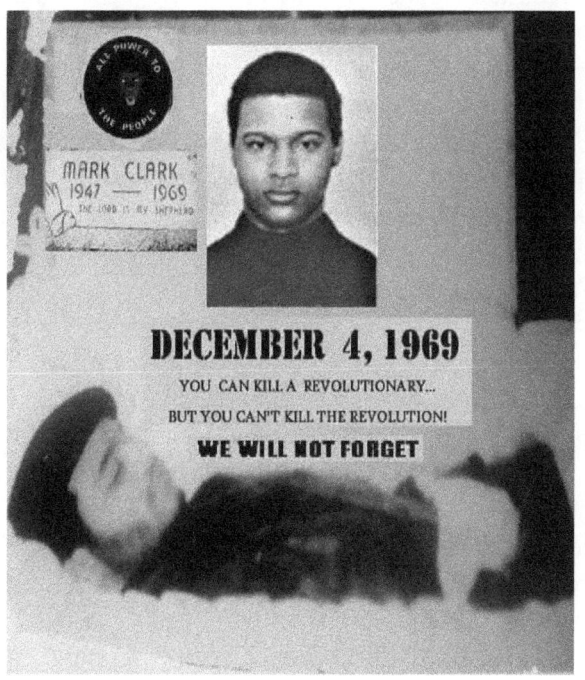

Mark Clark, Defense Captain of the Black Panther Party and Leader of the Peoria, Illinois Chapter

   Black Panther Party Leader, Mark Clark inspired inner-city youth and encouraged them to engage in struggle. He served the people and established community based-programs to meet the needs of the inner-city. The Peoria, Illinois Chapter of the Black Panther Party's Free

Breakfast Program was among the most prominent programs established. His commitment to struggle for the people, his courage as Defense Captain for the Black Panther Party, and his assassination December 4th 1969 along with Chairman Fred Hampton Sr. were significant events in the African American collective struggle for freedom. His legacy will forever be etched in our minds.

Mark Clark is part of a great family legacy with ancestral roots extending back to the African continent. His parents, the late couple, Elder William and Fannie Mae Clark are strong branches of an old ancestral tree. Their legacy includes seventeen children, and well over hundreds of grandchildren and great grandchildren; and their branches continue to extend. The Clark family members have not uncovered the stories of all their past ancestors. What they have learned is that they came from a lineage of strong people. From the time some of their ancestors left Virginia for the prairie lands of Eastern Mississippi and Western Alabama they were a strong family unit. Their children and children's, children became farmers, teachers, preachers, business owners, artists, poets, musicians, singers, entertainers, political activists and revolutionaries. Elder William and Fannie Mae Clark's seventh son, Defense

Captain Mark Clark was among the voices of revolution martyred in this country during modern times.

The year 2019 is an especially significant milestone year. It marks the 50th year since Elder William Clark Sr. passed away in 1969. It marks the 50th year anniversary of the December 4th 1969 raid and assassinations of the Black Panther Party Leaders, Defense Captain Mark Clark and Chairman Fred Hampton Sr. 2019 is an extra-significant milestone year marking the four hundredth year since the so-called 1619 Doctrine was established relegating black people to perpetual enslavement and underclass status.

According to scholars, the Africans that arrived in North America in 1619 aboard ships in Jamestown, Virginia were the first indentured servants or enslaved chattel. Whether this date and location are accurate, some may debate. One thing that is clear, from the moment black people were met with enslavement they resisted. From the taking over of slave ships, to the slave revolts of Denmark Vesey, Nate Turner's rebellion and other less known insurrections, black people have fought back and were willing to pay the ultimate price for freedom. These revolutionaries have always worked in conjunction with those willing to be co-workers in the cause of freedom.

In the nineteenth century, there were Abolitionist Movements working towards the abolishment of slavery. In the twentieth century there were religious leaders and Black Nationalist organizations such as the NAACP, SCLC, CORE, and SNCC, which emerged. These individuals and groups worked to improve social and economic conditions for black people; advancing the goals of revolutionaries. Many of the leaders of these organizations happened to be religiously affiliated. Among those who were influential in improving the conditions of black people in the twentieth century were Bishop Charles H. Mason Sr., The Most Honorable Elijah Muhammad, El Hajj Malik El Shabazz (Malcolm X), Minister Louis Farrakhan and Reverend Dr. Martin Luther King, Jr.

Reverend Dr. Martin Luther King Jr. was the glue that held together the Civil Rights Movement. Religious and secular groups, as well as activists and nationalists did not doubt his sincerity; even if they disagreed with his nonviolent approach. That may have been why

FBI Director J. Edgar Hoover deemed him the most dangerous. In hindsight, even Dr. King may have realized that integration contributed to the demise of the black business infrastructure. Once black people were afforded the legal rights to spend their money outside of their own communities, they stopped supporting black business. With Dr. King's charisma and influence he was able to pivot the Civil Rights Movement toward economic empowerment; synchronizing the message of economic justice among religious and nationalist groups. During the 1960s, for a brief moment in time; the Black Church, including Methodist, Baptist, Pentecostals, and Nation of Islam coordinated with grassroots activists, nationalists, revolutionaries toward a common goal.

Mark Clark's father, Elder William Clark Sr. was among the Pentecostal religious leaders who actively participated in implementing economic justice initiatives in the 1960's. His commitment to family, his exemplary fatherhood, and his efforts to improve the social and economic condition of the people established him among the influential religious leaders whose contributions should never be forgotten.

The year 2019 is an ensign to the nation. It is a time to reflect back on the movements and revolutions waged. It is a time to honor those who have dedicated their lives as servants of the people. Let us remember their sacrifices, reverence their memories, and look back at how far we have come as a people. As we observe the past, let us look forward to the future with hope, diligence, and steadfast determination to continue the struggle as co-workers for freedom until that day when a system of justice is finally established.

*To all our ancestors,
the enslaved Africans,
Indigenous, Aboriginals
and to those who have
lived and died fighting
for the causes of
Justice and Freedom,
I reverence and honor
your sacrifice. And say
Thank you*

*May your struggle for
the people and the
combined efforts of other
co-workers for freedom
which shall arise,
produce a
System of Justice!*

Rose (Clark) Morris

About The Author

Rose (Clark) Morris

Rose (Clark) Morris was born in Peoria, Illinois during the late 1950's. She is the seventeenth child born to Elder William Clark Sr. and Mother Fannie Mae Clark. As a child she watched her parents and siblings actively engaged in community service work. Her father was President of the Ministers Alliance, her older siblings joined the ranks of the NAACP, and her brother, Mark Clark became Defense Captain of the Black Panther Party and Leader of the Peoria, Illinois Chapter. Mark Clark educated his sister about African heritage and culture. His prompting sparked her interest in African History. Rose described her brother, saying "Mark exemplified the meaning of brotherly love".

After her father's sudden death in 1969, she moved to Flint, Michigan. That same year, her brother Mark was assassinated in Chicago, Illinois. The assassination and deaths traumatized her and she began suffering anxiety attacks. Rose found reading books relaxing and she immersed herself in her favorite subjects; African History, Kemetic History, and History of Pre-Western Civilizations. Eventually, she received several college degrees including a Bachelor of Science in Business Administration. She is a former Human Resources Manager who provided guidance to personnel in various manufacturing facilities, directed Benefits and Human Relations personnel in a regionally integrated health system, and provided leadership to various non-profit human services organizations. She was Interim Executive Director for a Michigan Housing Authority where she directed personnel working in new housing developments, senior apartment buildings, and low-income housing related service programs.

Rose has volunteered her time and expertise to support several of her favorite causes and organizations. She has worked as an Emergency Services Volunteer for a global humanitarian organization and she prepared meals at the local soup kitchen. She worked as a Substitute Teacher in the local school district where she helped educate students about the Civil Rights Movement and supervised an After School Enrichment Program. She has also served two terms as a member of the Office of Information System Advisory Board at the local college in Flint, Michigan.

Rose never forgot the experiences of her childhood. She became determined to tell the family stories and share how many of her family members actively participated in the struggle for civil rights. She attributes much of her family's active involvement in civil rights to their parents who were excellent role models. Her mother expressed her love thru her many hand-written letters to relatives and close friends. Each letter that Fannie Mae Clark wrote was carefully constructed to exhort and comfort its intended reader. Her mother's letters inspired her to write, although it took many years to understand just how important it was. As a child, her father allowed her to sit on the armrest in the front seat of his automobile and figure out which way they would turn next. His questions helped her stay alert and observe her surroundings; and figure out how to get from point A to point B". His training was invaluable and it helped her achieve a thorough understanding of map reading, geography, and where she was in this world".

Rose is extremely proud and beyond fortunate to have been born a member of the Clark family. Of her parents and siblings she proclaims, "To me, they are all African Kings, Queens, and High Priests because they walked in dignity and genuine love for the Great House".

In 2014, Rose and her family members were among those affected by the Flint Water

Crisis which occurred after a State-controlled Emergency Manager changed the water source to the Flint River. Thousands of men, women, and children were sickened with toxins like lead, E.coli, and legionella; some people died. Rose and all the other residents of Flint, Michigan continue to survive on bottled water.

In 2018, Rose (Clark) Morris completed her debut book, *Chronicle of the Seventh Son, Black Panther Mark Clark*. She currently lives in Flint, Michigan with her husband of twenty-two years. She has four adult children, six grandchildren, and many close relatives and friends.

References

Primary Book Sources

Civil Rights Chronicle, The African American Struggle for Freedom, By Bauerlein, Branham, Fertig, Burroughs, Carson, Forbes, Haskins, Lee, Lindsey, Podair, and Warner; Legacy Publishing 2003

Faith in Black Power: Religion, Race, and Resistance in Cairo, Illinois, 2016, by Kerry Pimblott

In Struggle, SNCC and the Black Awakening of the 1960's, 1981, by Claybourne Carson, Harvard University Press

Official Manual with the Doctrines and Discipline of the Church of God in Christ 1973; 1991 Edition, COGIC Publishing Board

Seize the Time: The Story of the Black Panther Party, (1969-1970),,by Bobby Seale

Southern Christian Leadership Conference Records, 1964-2012 (build 1968 – 2013) Stuart A. Rose Manuscript, Emery University

The Assassination of Fred Hampton, 2009, by Jeffrey Haas, Chicago Review Press

The Black Panther Party and the Case of the New York 21 by Annette T Rubenstein and Robert Rhodes, Lili Solomon, Janet Townsend; Charter Group for a Pledge of Conscience

The COINTELPRO Papers, 2001, by Churchill and Vander Wall

A Black Panther Retrospective Eerily Recalls the Present Day, by Kerry Cardoza, Nov. 2017, Chicagoreader.com

Internet Sources

All Power To The People, Discussion Guide. The Black Panthers, Vanguard of the Revolution, by Monifa Bandele and, Lumuba Bandele

Black Panthers and Fred Hampton; www.peopleslawoffice.com

Bishop Eleazar Lenox, Greater Holy Temple Church of God in Christ, www.GreaterHolyTemple.org

Mario Van Peebles Panther and Popular Memories of the Black Panther Party, 2007, by Kristen Hoerl, digital Commons @Butler University

Mark Clark's Body in Morgue Unclaimed: Family Never Notified; by Lawrence Maushard; The Community Word.com

Mark Clark and the Peoria Journal Star; by Lawrence Maushard; maushard.com

Mark Clark: Murdered During the Height of the Black Panther Party; blackthen.com; 8/16/2017

Mark Clark Legacy - The Life and Death of a Martyr; by The Root project; blog/myspace.com

Mark Clark: Return of the Black Panther Party., www.returnoftheblackpantherparty..webnode.com

Mason, Charles, Harrison, (1866-1961) The Black Past@BlackPast.org

Press Release - Mark Clark Memorial Tribute; by Kay Clark; Mark Clark Legacy webpage

Remember Fred Hampton and Mark Clark, www.freedomarchives.com

The Assassination of Fred Hampton and Mark Clark; itsabouttimebpp.com

The Open Assassination of Fred Hampton; by Joseph E. Green, radical.org

Magazines, Reports and Briefs

Federal Records Relating to Civil Rights in the Post World War II Era, 2006, National Archives and Records Administration, Washington D.C.

Hampton 7th Court of Appeals brief; Hampton v Hanrahan; 1973

Law Report Police Misconduct and Civil Rights Report: The Assassination of Fred Hampton 40 years later; by G. Flint Taylor and Ben H. Elson

Mom Files $3.75 Million Suit in Panther Son Killing June 25, 1970, Jet Magazine

Mom of Panther Sues Cops, State for $3 Million; October 15, 1970: Jet Magazine

Report by the Commission of Inquiry into the Black Panthers and the Police, by Roy Wilkens and Ramsey Clark, Commission Report

Roberts Temple Church of God in Christ, November 2005, Landmark Designation Report, Commission on Chicago Landmark's

Three Other Million dollar suits expected shortly; June 25, 1970, Jet Magazine

A Time to Act, Ebony Magazine, February 1970

The Kids Will Decide- And More Power To Them, Ebony Magazine, August 1970

Chicago Panthers file $28.6 Million Suit in U.S. Court, Jet Magazine, December 1970

Thesis and Dissertations

A Church where Jesus is Real, Race, Religiosity, and Legacies of Protest Activism in the Church of God in Christ 1968-1989, by Thom Finley, Brown University

Crossing the Color Line, The Church of God in Christ The Assemblies of God, and the Civil Rights Movement; by Blaine Charles Hamilton, Lee University, TN

Soul Power. The Black Church and the Black Power Movement in Cairo, Illinois 1969 -1974, by Kerry Louise Pimblott, University of Illinois, Urbana, Champaign

The Saints go Marching: The Church of God in Christ and the Civil Rights Movement in Memphis, Tennessee, 1954-1968 by Jonathan Chism, 2014, Rice University

Interviews

Matthew Clark
Dr. Patricia (Clark) Lewis

Newspapers and Periodicals

An Unfilled Prescription for Racial Equality, by Manly Howard, February 2008, Bay State Banner

Bishop Louis Ford, Leader in Civil Rights, by Kenan Heise, April 1995; Chicago Tribune

Bishop Louis Henry Ford, Head of the Church of God in Christ, April 1995; Los Angeles Times

Brotherly Love Can Kill You; Philly Pennsylvania Chapter; Feb. 1971; Black Panther Party Newspaper

Dead Man's Kin hopes Black Panthers film sends new message; by S. Salah, 1995, The Flint Journal

Harlem Church Where Malcolm X Eulogized Faces its own Final Days, NY Times

Luciano: Killing of Peorian Mark Clark at the Center of Black Panther; by Phil Luciano; 3/10/2018, P.J. Star.

Panther Clark Expected Death, Sister Reveals by Joseph Boyce, December 29, 1969, The Chicago Tribune

Panther Inquest, by Thomas J. Dolan, January 22, 1970, Chicago Sun Times

The Black Panther Raid and the Death of Fred Hampton. December 12, 1969, The Chicago Tribune

The Pantagraph: Jesse Jackson speaks at Illinois State University, Normal, Illinois, Newspaper, April 18, 1969

Audio Recording

That Niggers Crazy Album, Richard Pryor, Partee/Stax Records, 1974 (Part 3 re-released on YouTube

Martin Luther King Speaks. Our Victory Will be double, Matthew Siegfred, May 27, 2015 Youtube. (Illinois Wesleyan College Speech, February 1966)

I have been to the Mountaintop full speech. By Seur Jamz Ent., January 2013 Youtube (Last speech delivered at Mason Temple April 1968)

Secondary Book Sources

Face of Emmett Till; by M Till-Mobley; Dramatic Publishing

Going Down Jericho Road; by Michael K. Honey

Operation Breadbasket: An Untold Story of Civil Rights in Chicago, 1966-1971 by Martin L. Deppe and James Ralph, 2017, University of Georgia Press.

Soul on Ice, 1968; by Eldridge Cleaver

The Black Panthers Reconsidered, by Dr. Charles Jones, Georgia State University

The 1917 FBI Files of Bishop Charles Harrison Mason by Elijah L. Hill

The Trauma of Racism, 2015, by Lebron, Morrison, Ferris, Alcantara, Cummings, Parker and McKay, McSiver Institute for Poverty Policy and Research, New York University

The Quotations of Chairman Mao Tse-Tung; published by The Peoples Republic of China

www.ingramcontent.com/pod-product-compliance
Lightning Source LLC
Chambersburg PA
CBHW032138090426
42743CB00029B/670